Nancy D. Davis, MD
Ellen Cole, PhD
Esther D. Rothblum, PhD
Editors

Lesbian Therapists and Their Therapy: From Both Sides of the Couch

Pre-publication
REVIEWS,
COMMENTARIES,
EVALUATIONS . . .

"**T**his anthology illustrates the importance of personal psychotherapy in the development of clinical competence. The authors thoughtfully and practically address positive as well as negative aspects of their own therapy. They carefully examine the development of their own therapeutic styles in the wake of homophobia and/or boundary violations in their personal psychotherapy. This will serve as an important resource for trainees and clinicians alike."

Nanette K. Gartrell, MD
Associate Professor of Psychiatry
University of California, San Francisco

Harrington Park Press

Lesbian Therapists and Their Therapy: From Both Sides of the Couch

Lesbian Therapists and Their Therapy: From Both Sides of the Couch

Nancy D. Davis, MD
Ellen Cole, PhD
Esther D. Rothblum, PhD
Editors

Lesbian Therapists and Their Therapy: From Both Sides of the Couch, edited by Nancy D. Davis, Ellen Cole, and Esther D. Rothblum, was simultaneously issued by The Haworth Press, Inc., under the same title, as a special issue of the journal *Women & Therapy*, Volume 18, Number 2 1996, Esther D. Rothblum, and Marcia Hill, Editors.

Harrington Park Press
An Imprint of
The Haworth Press, Inc.
New York · London

1-56023-082-7

Published by

Harrington Park Press, 10 Alice Street, Binghamton, NY 13904-1580 USA

Harrington Park Press is an imprint of The Haworth Press, Inc., 10 Alice Street, Binghamton, NY 13904-1580 USA

Lesbian Therapists and Their Therapy: From Both Sides of the Couch has also been published as *Women & Therapy*, Volume 18, Number 2 1996.

The development, preparation, and publication of this work has been undertaken with great care. However, the publisher, employees, editors, and agents of The Haworth Press and all imprints of The Haworth Press, Inc., including The Haworth Medical Press and Pharmaceutical Products Press, are not responsible for any errors contained herein or for consequences that may ensue from use of materials or information contained in this work. Opinions expressed by the author(s) are not necessarily those of The Haworth Press, Inc.

Library of Congress Cataloging-in-Publication Data

Lesbian therapists and their therapy : from both sides of the couch / Nancy D. Davis, Ellen Cole, Esther D. Rothblum, editors.
     p. cm.
     Also . . . published as Women & therapy, volume 18, number 2, 1996 "–T.p. verso.
     Includes bibliographical references.
     ISBN 1-56024-800-9 (hbk. : alk. paper).–ISBN 1-56023-082-7 (pbk. : alk. paper)
     1. Lesbian psychotherapists. 2. Psychotherapist and patient. I. Davis, Nancy D. II. Cole, Ellen. III. Rothblum, Esther D.
RC440.84.L47 1996
616.89'14'086643–dc20
                                                        96-13471
                                                        CIP

INDEXING & ABSTRACTING

Contributions to this publication are selectively indexed or abstracted in print, electronic, online, or CD-ROM version(s) of the reference tools and information services listed below. This list is current as of the copyright date of this publication. See the end of this section for additional notes.

- *Abstracts of Research in Pastoral Care & Counseling*, Loyola College, 7135 Minstrel Way, Suite 101, Columbia, MD 21045
- *Academic Abstracts/CD-ROM*, EBSCO Publishing, P.O. Box 2250, Peabody, MA 01960-7250
- *Academic Index (on-line)*, Information Access Company, 362 Lakeside Drive, Foster City, CA 94404
- *Alternative Press Index*, Alternative Press Center, Inc., P.O. Box 33109, Baltimore, MD 21218-0401
- *CNPIEC Reference Guide: Chinese National Directory of Foreign Periodicals*, P.O. Box 88, Beijing, People's Republic of China
- *Current Contents: Clinical Medicine/Life Sciences (CC: CM/LS) (weekly Table of Contents Service), and Social Science Citation Index. Articles also searchable through Social SciSearch, ISI's online database and in ISI's Research Alert current awareness service*, Institute for Scientific Information, 3501 Market Street, Philadelphia, PA 19104-3302 (USA)
- *Digest of Neurology and Psychiatry*, The Institute of Living, 400 Washington Street, Hartford, CT 06106
- *Expanded Academic Index*, Information Access Company, 362 Lakeside Drive, Forest City, CA 94404
- *Family Studies Database (online and CD/ROM)*, Peters Technology Transfer, 306 East Baltimore Pike, 2nd Floor, Media, PA 19063
- *Family Violence & Sexual Assault Bulletin*, Family Violence & Sexual Assault Institute, 1310 Clinic Drive, Tyler, TX 75701
- *Feminist Periodicals: A Current Listing of Contents*, Women's Studies Librarian-at-Large, 728 State Street, 430 Memorial Library, Madison, WI 53706
- *Health Source: Indexing & Abstracting of 160 selected health related journals, updated monthly:* EBSCO Publishing, 83 Pine Street, Peabody, MA 01960
- *Health Source Plus: expanded version of "Health Source" to be released shortly:* EBSCO Publishing, 83 Pine Street, Peabody, MA 01960
- *Higher Education Abstracts*, Claremont Graduate School, 231 East Tenth Street, Claremont, CA 91711

(continued)

- *IBZ International Bibliography of Periodical Literature*, Zeller Verlag GmbH & Co, POB 1949, D-49009 Osnabruck, Germany

- *Index to Periodical Articles Related to Law*, University of Texas, 727 East 26th Street, Austin, TX 78705

- *INTERNET ACCESS (& additional networks) Bulletin Board for Libraries ("BUBL"), coverage of information resources on INTERNET, JANET, and other networks.*
  - JANET X.29: UK.AC.BATH.BUBL or 00006012101300
  - TELNET: BUBL.BATH.AC.UK or 138.38.32.45 login 'bubl'
  - Gopher: BUBL.BATH.AC.UK (138.32.32.45). Port 7070
  - World Wide Web: http: / / www.bubl.bath.ac.uk./BUBL/ home.html
  - NISSWAIS: telnetniss.ac.uk (for the NISS gateway)
  The Andersonian Library, Curran Building, 101 St. James Road, Glasgow G4 ONS, Scotland

- *Mental Health Abstracts (online through DIALOG)*, IFI/Plenum Data Company, 3202 Kirkwood Highway, Wilmington, DE 19808

- *PASCAL International Bibliography T205: Sciences de l'information Documentation*, INIST/CNRS-Service Gestion des Documents Primaires, 2, allee du Parc de Brabois, F-54514 Vandoeuvre-les-Nancy, Cedex, France

- *Periodical Abstracts, Research I* (general & basic reference indexing & abstracting data-base from University Microfilms International (UMI), 300 North Zeeb Road, P.O. Box 1346, Ann Arbor, MI 48106-1346), UMI Data Courier, P.O. Box 32770, Louisville, KY 40232-2770

- *Periodical Abstracts, Research II* (broad coverage indexing & abstracting data-base from University Microfilms International (UMI), 300 North Zeeb Road, P.O. Box 1346, Ann Arbor, MI 48106-1346), UMI Data Courier, P.O. Box 32770, Louisville, KY 40232-2770

- *Psychological Abstracts (PsycINFO)*, American Psychological Association, P.O. Box 91600, Washington, DC 20090-1600

- *Published International Literature on Traumatic Stress (The PILOTS Database)*, National Center for Post-Traumatic Stress Disorder (116 D), VA Medical Center, White River Junction, VT 05009

- *Sage Family Studies Abstracts (SFSA)*, Sage Publications, Inc., 2455 Teller Road, Newbury Park, CA 91320

- *Social Work Abstracts*, National Association of Social Workers, 750 First Street NW, 8th Floor, Washington, DC 20002

- *Studies on Women Abstracts*, Carfax Publishing Company, P.O. Box 25, Abingdon, Oxfordshire OX14 3UE, United Kingdom

(continued)

- *Violence and Abuse Abstracts: A Review of Current Literature on Interpersonal Violence (VAA)*, Sage Publications, Inc., 2455 Teller Road, Newbury Park, CA 91320

- *Women Studies Abstracts*, Rush Publishing Company, P.O. Box 1, Rush, NY 14543

- *Women's Studies Index (indexed comprehensively)*, G. K. Hall & Co., 866 Third Avenue, New York, NY 10022

SPECIAL BIBLIOGRAPHIC NOTES

related to special journal issues (separates)
and indexing/abstracting

☐ indexing/abstracting services in this list will also cover material in any "separate" that is co-published simultaneously with Haworth's special thematic journal issue or DocuSerial. Indexing/abstracting usually covers material at the article/chapter level.

☐ monographic co-editions are intended for either non-subscribers or libraries which intend to purchase a second copy for their circulating collections.

☐ monographic co-editions are reported to all jobbers/wholesalers/approval plans. The source journal is listed as the "series" to assist the prevention of duplicate purchasing in the same manner utilized for books-in-series.

☐ to facilitate user/access services all indexing/abstracting services are encouraged to utilize the co-indexing entry note indicated at the bottom of the first page of each article/chapter/contribution.

☐ this is intended to assist a library user of any reference tool (whether print, electronic, online, or CD-ROM) to locate the monographic version if the library has purchased this version but not a subscription to the source journal.

☐ individual articles/chapters in any Haworth publication are also available through the Haworth Document Delivery Services (HDDS).

CONTENTS

ABOUT THE EDITORS

Nancy D. Davis, MD, is a practicing psychiatrist who began her professional life in internal medicine. After 25 years of healing the body, she became a psychiatrist to heal the psyche. She is a life-long lesbian who has been in a joyous relationship with her partner for 47 years despite the rigors of medical practice.

Ellen Cole, PhD, is a psychologist and sex therapist and Professor of Psychology at Alaska Pacific University in Anchorage. A prolific writer, Dr. Cole has written and edited a variety of books, articles, and book chapters about women's health, including the long-term effects of sibling incest and sex at menopause. From 1985-1995, she co-edited the journal *Women & Therapy* and currently co-edits, with Esther Rothblum, the Haworth book program "Innovations in Feminist Studies." A current interest for Dr. Cole is "ecopsychology," a collaboration between psychologists and ecologists to reestablish connections between human beings and the nonhuman natural world.

Esther D. Rothblum, PhD, is Professor in the Department of Psychology, University of Vermont. Her research and writing have focused on lesbian mental health, and she is former chair of the Committee on Lesbian and Gay Concerns of the American Psychological Association. Esther has edited the books, *Loving Boldly: Issues Facing Lesbians,* and *Boston Marriages: Romantic but Asexual Relationships among Contemporary Lesbians.* She is currently working on a book on lesbians in academia with Beth Mintz.

FOREWORDS

The Quicksand of Boundary Violations

The collaboration of the three editors in producing this special volume has been especially valuable because each of us has come from such different backgrounds in age, culture, sexual orientation, and professional focus. Because of this welcome diversity, we have each written a foreword from our own perspective. Each of us represents of some portion of you, the readers. We wish it had been possible to have had more ethnic and racial diversity represented amongst the editors and authors, but our attempts to do this failed. We recognize that there are many more stories that need to be told to complete the picture of lesbian therapists and their own therapy.

I, Nan, conceived the idea of this special collection, with the belief that lesbian therapists are uniquely suited to comment on the special needs of lesbians in therapy from the vantage point of their own therapy. The response of the authors has been a surprise to me, in that many of them address boundary violations by their therapists. These boundary violations occurred with therapists who were male and female, and who were homosexual and heterosexual. This

[Haworth co-indexing entry note]: "The Quicksand of Boundary Violations." Davis, Nan D. Co-published simultaneously in *Women & Therapy* (The Haworth Press, Inc.) Vol. 18, No. 2, 1996, pp. xiii-xvi; and: *Lesbian Therapists and Their Therapy: From Both Sides of the Couch* (ed: Nancy D. Davis, Ellen Cole, and Esther D. Rothblum) The Haworth Press, Inc., 1996, pp. xiii-xvi; and: *Lesbian Therapists and Their Therapy: From Both Sides of the Couch* (ed: Nancy D. Davis, Ellen Cole, and Esther D. Rothblum) Harrington Park Press, an imprint of The Haworth Press, Inc., 1996, pp. xiii-xvi. Single or multiple copies of this article are available from The Haworth Document Delivery Service [1-800-342-9678, 9:00 a.m. - 5:00 p.m. (EST)].

xiii

adds fuel to the current discussions about boundary violations by professionals, which have caused the American Psychological Association, the American Psychiatric Association, and even the American Medical Association to reexamine their ethical positions on client/patient relationships. The trend towards becoming more stringent is clear, and this anthology reinforces that such changes are justified. Client-therapist sexual relationships are only the tip of the iceberg; there is more widespread damage caused by the misuse of the power of the therapist, as the articles in this book illustrate.

Another surprise for me was that so many of the therapists to whom I wrote seeking a contribution for this volume had not sought therapy themselves. A recent survey of psychologists (Pope and Tabachnick, 1994), reports that approximately 90% of women psychologists, and 94% of psychodynamic therapists, have been in therapy themselves. It was also noted that younger therapists were more likely to have been in therapy. It would seem, therefore, that the numbers of therapists who are doing therapy without having had personal therapy is on the wane. While this is the case for psychologists, it may not be true for psychiatrists who are much more likely these days to prescribe medication, rather than to combine medication with therapy. I personally mourn the passing of the psychiatrist who also has a good grounding in psychodynamic therapy from both sides of the "couch."

As clients ourselves, we have all experienced the power of the therapist in our lives, but statistics from the same survey emphasize this in an objective way. Of those who had finished therapy, 14% dreamed about and 31% daydreamed about a former therapist during the previous year. It is no surprise that the feelings of both client and therapist become sexualized; and it is very clear that damage to the client occurs when these feelings are acted out.

An interesting consideration is whether boundary violations are more common between lesbian clients and lesbian therapists than other types of therapeutic dyads. Certainly, there are greater problems in maintaining an appropriate distance when client and therapist are in the same lesbian community, but I know of many therapists who are, or have been, partnered by former clients, and many more who have made friends of former clients.

This book is dedicated to the therapeutic relationship: that sensitive state between two individuals which on the one hand allows sharing of the soul, but at the same time interdicts crossing of boundaries. Client and therapist must walk a fine line between emotional sharing and inappropriate sharing of their lives. Without the caring, true emotional change cannot take place, but with inappropriate caring, boundary violations are likely to take place. Therefore the healing relationship is only tissue paper's thickness away from being a harmful relationship if the client's boundaries are not fully honored by the therapist. As human beings, we, the therapists, want to have our own human needs met, as do our clients, and it is so easy for us to transgress client boundaries to fulfill our own unmet needs. The other side of this issue is not connecting sufficiently with our clients for us to be truly "with" our clients in an emotional sense, so they can have the security in which to explore their pain and to grow by the experience. We walk a tightrope, and it is a tribute to our balancing act that the therapeutic relationship is so often helpful, rather than harmful.

As women and lesbians, the therapeutic relationship is more easily tainted for us by sexism and homophobia from our male and heterosexual therapists than it is for male and heterosexual clients. Yet, there is the real risk of boundary violations from female and lesbian therapists who can relate to each other in special ways. The path of "good" therapy is fraught with pitfalls which must be dealt with by client and therapist alike, and when this is accomplished, the client can make great strides in learning how to be the wonderful and unique person she really is beneath all the pain.

This volume seeks enlightenment for the reader as to how to "pull off" this most difficult task of therapy in walking the line between the boundaries of client and therapist. By presenting our stories both as clients and as therapists, we hope the art of line walking will become clearer. It is as clients that we learn first (and probably best) about how the therapeutic process works. I believe that there is a real parallel between learning how we deal with life from our parents and learning how to conduct therapy from our therapists. If we, as clients, experience boundary violations, or lack of empathy, we are likely to repeat the same practices unless we have had the opportunity to process these experiences and gain perspective. When we are hurting in our own lives, it becomes very difficult to maintain the boundaries so necessary for a good outcome for the therapy. We all know this on an intellectual level. The hard part is practicing it, as it is so seldom a black and white issue.

I want to take this opportunity to thank Ellen Cole and Esther Rothblum, who as coeditors, enthusiastically accepted my proposal to edit this special collection on lesbian therapists and their own therapy. Their help and support enabled me to put together this volume, which I feel addresses so much that is not written by therapists, yet needs to be said in print. As therapists, I believe that we need to address our own feelings in the ways we ask our clients to do. It is a rare privilege for me to see my "brainchild" come to life under the able guidance of Esther and Ellen. I feel that I have been mentored by them in a way that says much about their feminist beliefs because they practice them. I shall be forever grateful to them for affording me this opportunity to help lesbian therapists speak of their personal experiences. I am also extremely grateful to the brave authors who were willing to expose themselves by sharing their feelings and lives in print.

The editing of this collection has been very gratifying to me, and is particularly meaningful to me as it occurs in the "sunset" of my professional life.

Nan D. Davis

REFERENCE

Pope, K.S., and Tabachnick, B.G. (1994). Therapists as patients: A national survey of psychologists' experiences, problems, and beliefs. *Professional Psychology: Research and Practice, 25,* 247-258.

When a Straight Psychologist Works
with Lesbian Clients

As a "straight" psychologist, I initially wondered if it was appropriate for me to work with Nan and Esther in co-editing this collection of articles about the personal therapy of lesbian therapists. The three of us agree, however, that I bring several important perspectives to this work. First, for the past 20 years, a quarter to a half of my therapy clients have been lesbians and lesbian couples. Second, as a straight woman, I represent a large percentage of probable readers and, in fact, helped to select and edit the following articles with these members of our audience in mind.

My sexual orientation or that of my therapists hasn't been a factor in my own therapy. The gender of my therapists, however, has been central. The first time I saw a therapist was in the mid-1960s. I was a 25-year-old doctoral student, my husband (now ex-husband) had left me for his secretary with whom he had been having an affair for several months, and I had a three-week-old baby. Although I had read and been very affected by *The Feminine Mystique*, its message hadn't yet sunk in. I insisted on seeing not only a male, not only a psychiatrist, but the chair of the Department of Psychiatry at the state university's medical school. I was into the omniscience of male authority in a big way.

Ten years later I was trained by Masters and Johnson in sex therapy. Their belief that "it takes a woman to understand another woman at the deepest, most subjective level" (and a man to understand a man) was by this time a passionately-held truth for me.

[Haworth co-indexing entry note]: "When a Straight Psychologist Works with Lesbian Clients." Cole, Ellen. Co-published simultaneously in *Women & Therapy* (The Haworth Press, Inc.) Vol. 18, No. 2, 1996, pp. xvii-xx; and: *Lesbian Therapists and Their Therapy: From Both Sides of the Couch* (ed: Nancy D. Davis, Ellen Cole, and Esther D. Rothblum) The Haworth Press, Inc., 1996, pp. xvii-xx; and: *Lesbian Therapists and Their Therapy: From Both Sides of the Couch* (ed: Nancy D. Davis, Ellen Cole, and Esther D. Rothblum) Harrington Park Press, an imprint of The Haworth Press, Inc., 1996, pp. xvii-xx. Single or multiple copies of this article are available from The Haworth Document Delivery Service [1-800-342-9678, 9:00 a.m. - 5:00 p.m. (EST)].

Since the days that I invested male authority figures with all that power, my own therapy has consisted of a homegrown variety of co-counseling–not the Harvey Jackins model, but one that a friend and I invented for ourselves. For 20 years, off and on, Jean and I met for two hours a week. For the first 45 or 50 minutes one of us was the counselor and the other the client. We spent the next 10 or 15 minutes "processing" the session, and then we'd reverse roles. We stopped only because I moved 3,000 miles away. Now I have a new co-counselor, and I shared with her Jean's and my system. Because we're both busily scheduled psychologists, we meet for only one hour a week. This means I now get to be the client every other week. No money is exchanged, and it works for us both. We improve as therapists, and we improve in the running of our lives. It feels like a very feminist process.

I believe I've been effective as a heterosexual therapist seeing lesbian clients. Because my husband and I have been fairly public in both towns in which we've lived, I generally assume that my lesbian clients know I'm straight. Nevertheless, when they tell me their sexual orientation, I tell them mine. I ask if that's okay. I ask them why they selected me, and one of the answers I often hear is that I'm known to be "gay-friendly."

"Gay-friendly," however, isn't enough. I've worked for many years, and continue to work, on my own consciousness-raising and homophobia. Conversely, I understand that we live in a homophobic world and that homophobia (both emanating from others and the internalized variety) is an issue for lesbians as well as heterosexuals. If my lesbian clients don't bring it up, I do. I inquire about the role of homophobia in their lives and find that, invariably, it exists for them as a problem, too.

I recall several painful but ultimately helpful incidents in which lesbian friends and colleagues challenged me for something I said that felt homophobic or insensitive to them. On one occasion I inadvertently and obliviously "outed" a friend. On another, at a business meeting with people I had never met before, I inquired about someone's sexual orientation. A lesbian colleague told me afterwards that she was horrified; that it wasn't an appropriate question. On reflection I understand that she was right.

I believe that everyone is born with some degree of bisexual potential, and I don't feel alienated from that part of myself. Recognizing my own bisexual potential allows me to empathize with my lesbian clients as easily as I might with heterosexual clients, and I believe that recognition is a crucial component for straight therapists who work with lesbian clients.

I continue to read widely in the lesbian and gay literature. From my reading and my clinical experience I've learned that coming out, even for the most "out" lesbian, is a process, and a frequently painful process. I've learned to be very sensitive to my clients' coming out stories and to recognize the depth of the pain that is often present.

Ironically, I have a few coming out stories of my own, although I'm aware they lack the devastating edge I've heard so often from clients. On one occasion I gave a speech at a medical conference in Utah about a research project I'd conducted on lesbians at menopause. When I left the podium I noticed a man pointing at me and heard him whispering to his neighbor, "She doesn't look like a lesbian." Throughout that weekend I wondered whether everyone assumed I was a lesbian, and whether or not I cared, and whether or not I should identify myself as straight.

On another occasion, my closest friend and I were hiking together in New Hampshire's Green Mountains, and as a treat to ourselves, we booked a room for one night at an establishment we'd seen advertised as a "women's inn." When we saw the couples hanging out in the lobby and noticed there was only one bed in each room, we quickly realized the patrons weren't just any women: they were lesbian couples, and the inn's ambiance was both beautiful and romantic. None of this was problematic for my friend and me until the communal breakfast the next morning. As the women at our table shared their lives (one couple had just gotten married–in a church–the previous day), with everyone assuming my friend and I were a couple, too, I felt increasingly like a fraud, or a spy. I was there, unwittingly, under false pretenses. We chose not to "come out" on that occasion, and still wonder whether or not we did the right thing.

As a sex therapist, I've learned that initiating sex can be hard for women, and when a couple consists of two women it can be doubly hard. Because sexual abuse is far more common for girls than it is for boys, it is likely that at least one partner in a lesbian relationship will have a history of child sexual abuse. For these reasons, and others, it is no wonder that we read and hear about lesbian "bed-death" and "Boston marriages." However, I also know many lesbian couples who have full and rich sex lives that are centrally important to the quality of their relationship. Therefore, I'm careful not to make assumptions about the sexual desires, needs, or fears of any lesbian or lesbian couple. Sexual histories and preferences differ from woman to woman, couple to couple. When a lesbian couple first sees me for sex therapy my job, above all, is to listen without judgment, evaluation, or preconceptions.

Although I tend to think a lesbian therapist might often be more appropriate than a straight therapist for a lesbian client, I've also recently wondered if there are any occasions in which a straight therapist might actually be preferable. Of course in many small towns there is no choice, but that's not what I'm wondering about here. I'm wondering if there might be any actual advantages, given a choice. Perhaps a lesbian client who isn't out or who's struggling with her own sexual identification might feel safer with a straight therapist. Such a woman might not even want to be seen in the waiting room of a known lesbian therapist, for of course without a feeling of immense safety I don't think therapy can work. Perhaps it could be safer, too, for a lesbian to address her own internalized homophobia with a straight therapist, without fear of judgment. And there's the simple (or not-so-simple) issue of chemistry. For some lesbian women, the very best fit might be with an aware, knowledgeable, and competent psychotherapist who also happens to be straight. I suspect this question warrants a paper of its own, or at least further consideration.

The anthology you are about to read is a very important one for straight therapists who see or might someday see lesbian clients. As straight psychotherapists, I think the most important thing we can do to enhance our sensitivity and our effectiveness in working with lesbians is to listen to them speak. It has been a privilege and an eye-opener for me to listen to the women who speak on the following pages.

Ellen Cole

Becoming a Lesbian Psychologist

Growing up, I can't recall ever knowing someone who was a therapist or who was in therapy. It would not have occurred to anyone in my family of origin to seek therapy in times of distress. Although my grandfather and Sigmund Freud had been classmates at the University of Vienna, no one in my immediate circle of friends had been to a psychoanalyst as a means of self-growth. When I came to the U.S. to go to college, I was aware that there was a counseling center on campus but knew of no one who had ever been there.

In hindsight, it is surprising to me that I chose to become a clinical psychologist. Although I was fascinated with human behavior, I had no interest in changing people. Even today, I teach diagnostics, not psychotherapy. I don't practice as a therapist.

During the first week of graduate school, my class was informed that we were required to be part of a "t-group." This was 1976, and prior classes of graduate students had advocated for some focus on feelings and process in their training to become clinicians. The t-group leader assigned to my class was a famous male psychologist who was also one of the most powerful faculty in the department. My classmates were tremendously flattered and excited. Classmates senior to us were envious and resentful. I was terrified. Although I had never been in a similar setting, I predicted that there would be pressure for us to self-disclose personal feelings and experiences. I had been attracted to girls since age six and I had never been attracted to or sexually involved with boys. I was falling in love

[Haworth co-indexing entry note]: "Becoming a Lesbian Psychologist." Rothblum, Esther D. Co-published simultaneously in *Women & Therapy* (The Haworth Press, Inc.) Vol. 18, No. 2, 1996, pp. xxi-xxv; and: *Lesbian Therapists and Their Therapy: From Both Sides of the Couch* (ed: Nancy D. Davis, Ellen Cole, and Esther D. Rothblum) The Haworth Press, Inc., 1996, pp. xxi-xxv; and: *Lesbian Therapists and Their Therapy: From Both Sides of the Couch* (ed: Nancy D. Davis, Ellen Cole, and Esther D. Rothblum) Harrington Park Press, an imprint of The Haworth Press, Inc., 1996, pp. xxi-xxv. Single or multiple copies of this article are available from The Haworth Document Delivery Service [1-800-342-9678, 9:00 a.m. - 5:00 p.m. (EST)].

xxi

with one of the women with whom I shared an apartment, and I couldn't stop talking about her. I was convinced that our famous professor–who was renowned for his clinical skills–would intuit this and I would be thrown out of graduate school as a result.

I still believe, in hindsight, that there would have been some serious consequences if knowledge of my lesbianism had leaked out. All the faculty but one were male and so were most of the graduate students. It was a very competitive, male-focused, homophobic setting. Although homosexuality had been removed as a diagnostic category from the DSM-II in 1973, the DSM-III did not appear in print until 1987.

The "real" t-group, it turned out, was when the other two female graduate students and I got together to discuss what we should and shouldn't say in the whole group. Of course I didn't mention that I was a lesbian, but at least I had routine discussions with the other two women in my class and we were unified in our concerns about self-disclosure. The famous male psychologist, not surprisingly, was not the clairvoyant I had feared he would be. In fact, he had difficulty getting any of us to say much of importance during our weekly group meetings. By this time even the male graduate students had realized that anything too personal they said might work against them at a later point. The professor's strategy was to become tremendously self-disclosive himself, mostly about other faculty in the department and about his deteriorating relationship with his wife. I remember feeling a sense of sisterhood with his wife when she would knock on his door to give him a ride home after the group meetings.

At least no one affiliated with my graduate program knew I was a lesbian and so I was not at risk of someone blowing my cover. Two lesbian friends of mine at the time were in another graduate program, and they had told their roommate (also a graduate student) that they were a couple. The roommate and one of the lesbians were in a required t-group similar to the one I was in. Each week, the roommate would threaten to disclose their lesbian relationship because she felt it was important that the t-group knew about important personal relationships. Each week my friends (one who was in the group and one who was waiting at home) would cope with the uncertainty and fear.

Therapy was not an option when I was a graduate student–I didn't have the money. Most of the therapists in the university town where I was living had been trained at my university, and probably were still connected with my professors or even supervised by them. I assume that had I gone to therapy at that time, my being a lesbian would have been pathologized and there would have been some attempt at "re-orientation."

By the time I was doing my post-doctoral fellowship at Yale University in 1980, some communities had their first openly identified lesbian therapists. This was the case in New Haven. As Charles Silverstein has described in his book *Gays, Lesbians, and Their Therapists* (1991), these were of the first "generation" of lesbian therapists. Typically they had no formal training in "mainstream" graduate programs but this was fine with the lesbian community, who had no respect for therapists trained in patriarchal, heterosexist models anyway. These therapists knew about feminism and they were part of the lesbian community–too much a part of it, often. Laura Brown (1988) has written about how most communities seemed to have one "therapy cult" centered around a therapist with poor boundaries who was often sexually involved with clients, living with clients, or who employed clients in her business. These therapists were not licensed or credentialed and they weren't covered by health insurance, but then no lesbian I knew in New Haven in 1980 had health insurance. Before I knew my first openly lesbian lawyer, doctor, dentist, or vet–professions that require more traditional training–I knew of lesbian therapists.

By the time I began my faculty appointment at the University of Vermont in 1982, much had changed. There were a dozen or so other lesbian faculty with whom I socialized. Their lovers and friends were lesbian doctors and lawyers as well as blue collar workers and community activists. Lesbians were making it through training and employment in mainstream jobs at all income levels, and they were doing so openly. In many ways, this second generation was still suffering the indignities of overt sexism and heterosexism in their training and in the workplace, and they often changed these institutions so that the next generation had a markedly different climate that was more accepting of lesbians.

The reason I first went to therapy in 1983 was that I was ending a relationship, and I wanted to talk to someone who would keep my conversations confidential. The only out lesbian therapist in town at that time was not credentialed–I don't think she had even completed her undergraduate college degree–but she had years of therapy experience with lesbians and she could accept my Blue Cross health insurance at the time (how things have changed!). Sitting in her waiting room was a social experience, as many of my close friends and acquaintances went to her as well.

The 1980s were a time when lesbians went to therapy. When Kris Morgan (1992) distributed flyers at a women's basketball game inviting spectators to participate in a survey, 100 lesbians and 309 heterosexual women agreed to participate. In this sample, 77.5% of the lesbians and 28.9% of the heterosexual women had been in therapy–an enormous difference. On the Attitudes Toward Seeking Professional Psychological Help Scale (Fischer & Turner, 1970), lesbians scored higher than heterosexual women on the subscales Recognition of Personal Need, Tolerance of Stigma, Confidence in the Mental Health Profession, and Counseling as Growth. In a later study, Kris Morgan and Michele Eliason (1992) interviewed 23 lesbians who had been and 17 lesbians who had never been to therapy, and found that both groups viewed lesbians to be introspective and saw the lesbian communities as valuing personal growth. Celia Kitzinger and Rachel Perkins (1993) have critiqued this phenomenon in their book *Changing Our Minds*. They argue that psychological terminology (e.g., the "inner child") has replaced political activism in the lesbian communities, and that therapy privatizes and individualizes lesbians' lives. At the same time, there are few resources for lesbians undergoing serious long-term mental health problems and they argue for lesbian communities to organize around sharing resources for long-term caregiving.

As I write this in 1994, there are well over 20 lesbian therapists in my town, although their degree of outness varies. They are psychiatrists, psychologists, social workers, and counselors. There are dozens of heterosexual therapists who are well trained in working with lesbians, lesbian couples, children of lesbians, and parents of lesbians. I have been to therapy (with a lesbian therapist) since my first therapy experience, and it never would have occurred to me to worry that any aspect of being a lesbian would be pathologized.

Five graduate students are currently doing their dissertations on lesbian issues under my supervision. I am out in all my classes, in my research and writing, to my family, friends, and colleagues, and students. At the same time, health benefits (including mental health benefits) are being sharply reduced and therapists are beginning to feel the effects. The Republican controlled congress and senate, especially at a time of economic hardship, may fuel anew the homophobic attitudes and behaviors that my generation of lesbians worked hard to eradicate.

The accounts that follow illustrate that combination of persistence in the face of blatant heterosexism, with occasional sensitivity on the part of even the most traditional of therapists, that was the experience of lesbian therapy clients not too long ago. Because the clients themselves became therapists (sometimes *because* of their experiences as lesbian clients) they have the advantage of being able to examine their own therapy experiences from the vantage point of trained professionals. Their accounts describe how being a lesbian has affected their own therapy–as a client and as a therapist. We would like to thank the authors that follow for their honesty and their insights. Their experiences, in part, have made it possible today for lesbian therapists-in-training–as well as lesbian clients–to experience a more affirmative therapy.

Esther D. Rothblum

REFERENCES

Brown, L.S. (1988). Beyond thou shalt not: Thinking about ethics in the lesbian feminist community. *Women & Therapy, 8,* 13-26.

Fischer, E.H., & Turner, J.Le.B. (1970). Orientations to seeking professional help: Development and research utility of an attitude scale. *Journal of Consulting and Clinical Psychology, 35,* 79-90.

Kitzinger, C., & Perkins, R. (1993). *Changing our minds: Lesbian feminism and psychology.* NY: New York University Press.

Morgan, K.S. (1992). Caucasian lesbians' use of psychotherapy. *Psychology of Women Quarterly, 16,* 127-130.

Morgan, K.S., & Eliason, M.J. (1992). The role of psychotherapy in Caucasian lesbians' lives. *Women & Therapy, 13,* 27-52.

Silverstein, C. (1991). *Gays, lesbians, and their therapists.* NY: W.W. Norton.

ARTICLES

When a Therapist Breaks the Rules

G. Dorsey Green

SUMMARY. This article chronicles Dr. Green's experiences as a client in Seattle between November, 1977 and May, 1979. The history includes how the author came to find this particular therapist, the therapist's cutting the author off from family and friends, the shift to a friendship relationship, co-owning a business and being a co-therapist with the therapist and her partner, the disentangling of the whole mess and the aftereffects of that time spent as her client. There is a discussion at the end of the article of how this experience has affected the author's work as a lesbian feminist therapist who does primarily long-term therapy.

Recently, Dr. Green has seen more clients who have been damaged by their lesbian feminist therapist. Much of this damage has been done by the slow erosion of boundaries which separate thera-

G. Dorsey Green has a PhD in Counseling Psychology. She practices as a therapist, consultant, and writer in Seattle, WA. She is the co-author with D. Merilee Clunis of *Lesbian Couples* (1988) and *Lesbian Parenting* (1995).

The author thanks Ann Stever for her support and editorial suggestions.

[Haworth co-indexing entry note]: "When a Therapist Breaks the Rules." Green, G. Dorsey. Co-published simultaneously in *Women & Therapy* (The Haworth Press, Inc.) Vol. 18, No. 2, 1996, pp. 1-10; and: *Lesbian Therapists and Their Therapy: From Both Sides of the Couch* (ed: Nancy D. Davis, Ellen Cole, and Esther D. Rothblum) The Haworth Press, Inc., 1996, pp. 1-10; and: *Lesbian Therapists and Their Therapy: From Both Sides of the Couch* (ed: Nancy D. Davis, Ellen Cole, and Esther D. Rothblum) Harrington Park Press, an imprint of The Haworth Press, Inc., 1996, pp. 1-10. Single or multiple copies of this article are available from The Haworth Document Delivery Service [1-800-342-9678, 9:00 a.m. - 5:00 p.m. (EST)].

1

pist from client. It is this erosion and subsequent exploitation that the author explores in her article. *[Article copies available from The Haworth Document Delivery Service: 1-800-342-9678.]*

I moved to Seattle in June, 1977 to begin graduate school in Counseling Psychology and for my partner, Margaret, to do her internship in Osteopathic Medicine. We knew no one. I was 27 years old, white, and from an upper-middle class background. I had grown up on the Eastern Shore of Maryland, living eight miles outside of a town of 10,000 people. My parents were divorced when I was 13, and my mother had died unexpectedly when I was 24. My father and his family still lived in Maryland. I had little familiarity with a city like Seattle and less experience with therapists.

While this is not the usual way to begin a journal article, I think that it is important to explain the context in which I began therapy with Marta (not her real name). I will describe how my relationship with this therapist evolved, the immediate aftermath, and the long-term effects of that year-and-a-half. I will also talk briefly about how this experience has affected my work as a therapist. This is my story of pain and healing, the more powerful because of the value I place on the therapeutic relationship.

EVOLUTION OF THE THERAPEUTIC RELATIONSHIP

When Margaret and I had been in Seattle for a few months, she left for a three-month rotation in a small hospital three hours from Seattle, and I began graduate school. We planned to see each other every weekend. Within a month Margaret and I had a crisis which threatened our relationship.

I asked around for a therapist who knew how to work with lesbian couples. In 1977, in Seattle, there were very few out lesbian therapists or heterosexual therapists who had much familiarity with lesbians. I interviewed one who stumbled over the word homosexual and never said lesbian. My search eventually led me to Marta, one of the few therapists who was known to work with lesbians.

Her lover, Carol (not her real name), met us at the door and took us down to Marta's office in the basement of their house. Marta interviewed us and agreed to see us. She had a number of years of experience as a therapist, had good recommendations, and was available. She was pleasant and seemed to know what she was doing. We needed help and decided to see her. She said she wanted Carol to be a second therapist in our sessions. We did not know at the time that Carol had been Marta's client before they became lovers and that Marta continued to treat Carol as a client when they thought it was necessary, even while they lived together.

Marta was a very charismatic and talented therapist. She rapidly sorted out Margaret's and my initial problem. Soon both Margaret and I were seeing Marta for individual as well as couples therapy. I fell into the habit of visiting with Carol before and after my individual sessions and enjoyed her company a lot. I had made only one real friend at school and badly missed my friends in the east and Midwest.

After Margaret had been back in Seattle full-time for a few months, one of the four of us initiated spending social time together. Within a very short time we were the best of friends. We spent all of our social time with Marta and Carol and I stopped being lonely. Margaret also began to have a physician-patient relationship with both women. Margaret is a very talented Osteopathic Physician, specializing in manipulative medicine. They loved having Margaret take care of them and we loved being able to give something back to these two women who were helping us.

A few months after starting therapy with Marta, she asked us to join a group she planned to run for lesbian couples. We were one of five couples, most of whom saw Marta for individual therapy as well. Many of those women also became our friends. When Marta and Carol had a Valentine's Day party, our group was there, along with other clients. All of us loved her.

One of the hallmarks of Marta's therapy was her focus on clients' family members. It appeared to me as if Marta encouraged most of her clients to break contact with one or more friends or family. She told Margaret and me to break off communication with the family member closest to each of us. It was as if only Marta and her circle of friends were good enough for any of us "special clients." In fact, she was even beginning to drive a wedge between Margaret and me. By Spring, 1978, Marta and Carol had taken me into their confidence about how "mentally ill" Carol was; they told me not to tell Margaret. I was being "trained" by Marta to help in Carol's treatment.

Margaret and I spent the summer away from Seattle and away from Marta. When we got back I was not sure I wanted to do any more therapy. I felt fine and something felt "funny" to me about Marta's work. I raised this at my first session with her and before I knew it I was crying and in need of therapy again. And so, we resumed our relationship.

Somewhere during this fall, Marta decided that Margaret was not good for me. Marta began to cut Margaret out of some of the socializing and eventually told Margaret she needed to be just a client for awhile. We believed her. A month or two later Carol and Marta invited her to rejoin the three of us as friends again, at a time which seems to have coincided with their need for her osteopathic care.

Early in 1979 Marta invited me to co-lead a therapy group with her. She recruited about five of her individual clients for it and we began to meet weekly. We also saw a couple together as co-therapists. I was flattered and thrilled that this wonderful therapist had chosen me to follow in her footsteps. I thought we were on the cutting edge of how to do good therapy. I insisted that I not do therapy as a client with Marta while we led the group together and she agreed. I struggled to ignore the comments I was beginning to hear from other therapists about Marta's history of "doing dirt" to her colleagues. Marta always had a good reason why those "other" folks deserved what she had done to them and I willingly took her side.

Interestingly, the ending of my relationship with Marta began with our work in the group together. I noticed that she forced people out of therapy if they did not agree with what she told them to do. She had told me about past clients who had "quit," but Marta had always had "sound therapeutic explanations." Now I could see that she was rigid and controlling. Whenever one of her clients quit, the rest of us knew that the ex-client was off limits. We should not talk to "those women." There was definitely an insider group and the rest of the world.

The other reason for the disintegration was that Marta, Margaret,

Carol and I bought a tavern together. We owned it for a little over a month before the trouble began. From the very beginning Margaret and I expressed some disagreements with Marta about how she was doing things; this was a marked difference from our previous behavior. The breaking point came when Margaret refused to serve wine to a diabetic man who was an alcoholic. He had told Margaret that he had almost died because he had gotten drunk. She told him she would not serve him because she cared about him. Marta was furious at Margaret. I think now that Marta knew she was not in charge anymore and that she needed to get rid of us.

As the tavern trouble was heating up, I was getting depressed. I was beginning to realize that Marta was not as good a therapist as I had thought and was not a trustworthy business partner. I was completely dependent on her for my social life and much of my money was tied up in the tavern. I began to shut down emotionally. Marta told me that I was "crazy" and that I had to start therapy with her again and take a leave from running the group. I agreed and we decided to tell the group the next Monday night. I began the group by explaining I was having a difficult time in my personal life and needed to take a month or two off and that I would return after that. Marta stopped me and said that she had changed her mind; she never wanted to work with me again. She went on to say that she had asked all her clients to trust me and that I had betrayed that trust. I cannot recall how I was supposed to have done that but almost everyone in the group believed her. Marta then invited me to join the group as a participant, since I obviously needed the help. I was thrown to the women in the group as a sacrifice and they attacked with gusto. Some called me names and others simply said they were glad to see me go. Years later one woman told me that she decided to quit the group that night. She figured that if Marta would do that to me, she could go after anyone.

Later that night Marta asked Margaret and me to sell her our share of the tavern; she proposed an amount to pay us. She said she was sickened by us, that we clearly needed help and she would see us as clients only. We left and went home. I was numb and my memory is a little fuzzy about the next hour or so. I do remember that Margaret was furious and she galvanized us into action. We decided to go over to the tavern the next morning and take all of our personal possessions. We had a hunch we would have only one chance. We also had some things at Marta and Carol's house and their house key. We went there as well, gathered our belongings and left the key. It proved to be our only opportunity to take back what we had loaned them. Marta and Carol were never willing to discuss with us the few things we had not been able to find.

The flurry of ending our relationships with Marta and Carol left me depressed and scared. I did not trust myself and was having trouble doing my graduate work. I was worried that Carol would come "get us" and hurt us. She had a Black Belt in Karate and Marta had always made us aware of how dangerous Carol was. There had always been a covert understanding that Carol might hurt people who hurt Marta. I was terrified.

In the early summer I started to see a therapist named Patricia. Although I do not remember Patricia's ever saying the word depression, she clearly treated me for it. And it was with her that I finally found my anger.

Later that summer we heard from Marta. She sent us a proposal confirming her offer to buy out our share of the tavern and settling other debts. It was ludicrous! She was charging us for tavern logo jackets we had ordered (but never got) before she had broken off our relationships and for a therapy session I was supposed to have had the morning after my last group session.

Patricia, who had heard of Marta and had thought her to be a reputable therapist, encouraged me to engage with Marta and explain my disagreements with her accounting. Marta called and asked if I had received the proposal. She told me that all her friends thought that the amount she had offered for our share of the tavern was way too generous and we should be grateful. When I challenged the charges she was subtracting from the tavern settlement, she got furious and told me I should talk to an attorney if I wanted to do anything different. Even though my stomach was churning and my legs shook, I finally had a glimmer of how inappropriate this woman was. Marta said she had begun the legal process of buying the tavern from us and the escrow people would contact me. I realized she was assuming I would just accept her proposal and I said I would think about it. If I continued to have questions I would have my attorney contact her. She hung up on me. When I repeated this conversation to Patricia, she was amazed. She was beginning to understand Margaret's and my experience.

The ending of our legal relationship with Marta was in character. She completed the paperwork necessary to buy our share of the tavern and the escrow company called me to sign. They told me Marta had not signed yet and because of that they could not release the check to me. I called Marta to tell her I was ready and to ask when she would sign. She countered by saying she was very busy and leaving in a day for a two-week trip and she did not think she could get to it. When I relayed this to the escrow representative she scoffed and said she would call Marta. The woman called me back and said that Marta had been very pleasant and had agreed to sign the payment release on her way out of town. Marta did not keep that appointment.

Now it was my turn to be furious. Margaret and I consulted an attorney who said that as legal owners we were liable for what went on in the tavern, even if we had nothing to do with the day-to-day operations. He called the escrow company and told them his clients were very concerned about the liability and that we would surrender the tavern license if they did not process the sale and give us our money. Surrendering a license shuts a tavern down for an unknown amount of time. Marta would lose much money and have to explain herself back into another license. I admit to a moment of glee as we contemplated that move but I wanted my money and freedom more. The escrow officer capitulated and said he thought he could release the check, he was sure Marta would want it that way.

AFTERMATH

I worked in therapy with Patricia for about two years. Most of my work centered around recognizing my feelings and looking at the vulnerabilities which contributed to my getting caught up by Marta. I am forever grateful to Patricia for helping me find myself and for believing that I was not crazy. Sometimes as therapists it is difficult to know when a client is creating the problem with an ex-therapist out of anger and when the client has been damaged by a therapist.

Marta's violation of almost all therapeutic boundaries contributed to my gradually losing my sense of who I was. At the same time I felt special, privileged, and cared for. My eyes tear up re-membering those feelings. I ache for the person I was, who so longed to be loved that way. I know that I am not unique in these feelings and unfortunately, I am not unique in my experiences.

When I was at APA a number of years ago I heard Phillip Zim-bardo's talk on cults. He was describing Jonestown and the tragedy that took place there. My memory is that he defined real brainwash-ing as the ability to get someone to believe and do what you want them to do, even when you, the enforcer, are not present. My expe-rience with Marta was similar. I really believed what she told me *and* I recruited others to be clients as well.

It took me a long time not to be scared that Marta and Carol would retaliate. I was frightened for my physical safety and I worried that Marta could hurt me professionally. It was a relief when I realized she was not respected in the feminist therapy community in Seattle. I also learned that other therapists had wanted to get to know me but were put off by my association with Marta. Worry about safety and reputation is not uncommon for some survivors of abusive therapy. It depends on how much threat, covert or overt, was used. Marta actu-ally told one client that she would die if she quit therapy.

Many years later I received a subpoena to appear in court. Carol was suing Marta for violating therapeutic boundaries. I was being asked to testify that Marta had told me she had used an electric cattle prod on Carol during therapy sessions. I had known that testifying was a possibility and was not completely surprised, but I went into shock. It took two weeks for me to get grounded again. With my therapist I worked on my terror, my shame, and my deci-sion about whether I would go to court. Testifying was very hard. I worried that people would think I was a dependent wimp or that Marta's attorney would do something to make me look foolish. By the end I felt brave and glad to have testified. I felt strong that I had finally taken my soul back, with Marta sitting there.

EFFECTS ON MY PRACTICE

In the sixteen years since my relationship with Marta I have thought much about what happened in that year-and-a-half. I have seen several clients who were abused and damaged by other therapists. Their stories eerily echo my own experience and also have differences which reflect their individual vulnerabilities and their therapist's particular style.

Clients report feeling crazy when they try to explain how they got so enmeshed with this kind of therapist. As I write this, I am embarrassed about how much I allowed Marta to take over my life. I lost all sense of what was appropriate therapeutic behavior. I cut myself off from friends and I stopped trying to make new friends. My world focused on Marta, Carol, and our time together. When clients talk about their sense of shame at having been taken in or abused by a therapist, I understand.

With 20/20 hindsight, I can see what made my relationship with Marta so destructive. During the experience, I did not see my increasing dependence and isolation, nor did I see Marta's need for control. Looking back, I see Marta's lack of boundaries in her relationship with Carol, her encouragement of inappropriate socializing between the four of us as well as other clients, her isolating us from other friends and family, and even an attempt to split us off from each other. When either Margaret or I had a nagging feeling something was wrong, we did not honor it.

It is clear to me that almost anyone can be seduced by a therapist if she or he is vulnerable enough at the right time. Whether the seduction is sexual or not is not the major factor, the stories are similar. There is a building of trust and some real therapeutic help in the early stages. Then the client is made to feel special. Often the therapist will acknowledge that she or he is proposing some unorthodox behavior, whether it be sex, friendship, or a business relationship. The therapist always has "good" reasons for "breaking the rules." There is often the threat of abandonment if the client wants to go against the therapist's plan and it takes a great deal of courage for a client to break away from this type of relationship.

Many people do not talk about their experiences because of their shame. We have been raised in this culture to value independence, and to admit that we became so dependent can be very difficult. When this dependence is abused so badly, our shame, pain, embarrassment, fear, anger, and disorientation get all intertwined. It can be extraordinarily difficult to risk opening up to another therapist in the hopes of gaining some peace and healing.

My practice as a therapist has definitely been affected by my history with Marta. I carry always an awareness of a client's vulnerability and how important it is for me to maintain clear and respectful boundaries. I work hard to create a safe place where clients can feel safe and understood. I also appreciate the necessity of challenging people to struggle with the troublesome aspects of themselves and their lives. Unless I both support and challenge my clients, I believe that I can inadvertently invite dependency that is stultifying instead of dependency which leads toward healing and growth. Marta offered me a warm place to hide if I was willing to give myself away. It was not a kind offer. I want my clients to know that they can be safe while they stay and do their work and they can leave with my support and blessing when they are ready.

Personal Therapy
of One Lesbian Therapist:
A Lesson in Power and Responsibility

Maryka Biaggio

SUMMARY. During my early adulthood I sought therapy at a university counseling center. As a result of my therapist's recommendation I attempted, unsuccessfully, to adopt a heterosexual lifestyle. That therapy experience had a great impact on my early adult years and on my professional development and outlook. My understanding of how I was influenced by this therapy experience helped shape my professional views about the therapist's power and responsibility vis-à-vis the client. These views have in turn influenced my approach to educating clinical psychologists: I believe it is important to instill in students an understanding of the power we have over clients and the incredible burden of responsibility that our professional role carries with it. *[Article copies available from The Haworth Document Delivery Service: 1-800-342-9678.]*

During my early adulthood, while attending undergraduate college, I experienced a sense of confusion and distress, and began to

---

Maryka Biaggio, PhD, is Professor in the School of Professional Psychology, Pacific University, 2004 Pacific Avenue, Forest Grove, OR 97116. She oversees admission to the graduate program and teaches Psychology of Women. She is also active in the Association for Women in Psychology.

[Haworth co-indexing entry note]: "Personal Therapy of One Lesbian Therapist: A Lesson in Power and Responsibility." Biaggio, Maryka. Co-published simultaneously in *Women & Therapy* (The Haworth Press, Inc.) Vol. 18, No. 2, 1996, pp. 11-17; and: *Lesbian Therapists and Their Therapy: From Both Sides of the Couch* (ed: Nancy D. Davis, Ellen Cole, and Esther D. Rothblum) The Haworth Press, Inc., 1996, pp. 11-17; and: *Lesbian Therapists and Their Therapy: From Both Sides of the Couch* (ed: Nancy D. Davis, Ellen Cole, and Esther D. Rothblum) Harrington Park Press, an imprint of The Haworth Press, Inc., 1996, pp. 11-17. Single or multiple copies of this article are available from The Haworth Document Delivery Service [1-800-342-9678, 9:00 a.m. - 5:00 p.m. (EST)].

put labels on my ongoing experience of differentness. It was during this time that I sought therapy at the university counseling center. That therapy experience made a great impression on me at the time and subsequently had a great impact on my early adult years and on my professional development and outlook. This therapy experience was a little over 20 years ago, however, and my memory is less than complete. But I do remember the outlines of my experiences in and out of therapy, along with some key events which made enough of an impression on me to stay with me over the years.

The most memorable and, I think, most consequential event in my therapy related to exploration of concerns about my sexual orientation. I was genuinely distressed and confused at this time, and probably wasn't even sure exactly why. But I know that I did reveal my feelings of attraction for women, and my fears that I might be a lesbian. My therapist's reaction to our discussion was something to the effect that "It's OK to be a lesbian, but not if it's because you are afraid of men, and you need to deal with your fear of men."

What was the immediate effect of this interpretation or recommendation on my life? I began to date men, and tried to squelch my feelings of attraction toward women. Soon thereafter, I entered into a relationship with a man who was somewhat older, and I lived with him for two years. Gradually, my continuing feelings of attraction toward women, my developing sense of personal strength, and my awareness that lesbianism was a viable lifestyle led me to end this relationship. I had another therapy experience within the next several years, gradually came to terms with my sexual orientation and internalized homophobia, connected with a supportive lesbian feminist community, and went on to comfortably identify as a lesbian. I also attended graduate school, earned a doctorate in psychology, and began an academic career and psychology practice. In recent years I have had occasion to look back on my therapy experience, assessing both its impact on my personal life and my professional development. I'd like to explain in this paper how it was that this therapy experience was so consequential, and how it has affected my professional views.

THE THERAPY EXPERIENCE:
THE SOCIAL CONTEXT (1969-1973)

I obviously took my therapist's recommendation or interpretation seriously, making a major life decision on the basis of it. Why did I do this? In retrospect I feel this was a naive, even stupid, thing for me to do. If I were in therapy now I would certainly not take a therapist's suggestion so literally. But I am a different person now, and I acted as I did at that time because of who I was then.

In order to explain how easily influenced I was by my therapist I must describe the social context and the perspective which I brought to the therapy experience. I attended undergraduate school from 1969-1973, a time of social ferment. I identified with the Vietnam protest movement and the youthful rebellion against contemporary American values. I associated with a peer group which shared these views and provided some sense of identity and validation. But this was a time when one's sense of self was certainly a shifting and ill-defined entity–if one did not identify with the prevailing cultural values and did not foresee following the recognized path of adult development, then where did one fit and what was one's path?

In addition to this general confusion about identity, I was struggling with anxieties and fears about my sexual orientation. I grew up in a Catholic household where discussions about sexuality, to say nothing of homosexuality, were taboo. I was privy to the usual derogatory comments from peers about "queers," "faggots," and "dykes." So I grew up fearing homosexuality, and believing that homosexuals were a depraved lot. Still, as I reached early adulthood, my feelings of differentness and attraction toward women persisted. In fact, my own personal questioning was in part responsible for my interest in psychology. I declared myself a psychology major from the beginning of college, and sifted through psychology writings for anything I could find about homosexuality. I don't remember what authors I read, but I do remember being left with the impression that homosexuality was an abnormal aberration, even a perversion. So, upon entering therapy, I was afraid of my sense of differentness, and was operating under the impression that homosexuality was perverse.

The therapist to whom I was assigned was a young man who had recently graduated from a university with an impressive name. I ascribed much expert authority to my therapist, and believed that he could help me. My parents had imbued me with a great respect for education, and I regarded well-educated persons with some awe. My therapist was relaxed in his demeanor, seemed to be politically progressive, and even had a beard. These hints of "hippie" tendencies led me to feel some identification with him. This man was very caring and concerned about the distress I recounted, and I came to trust him.

Given my own distress and confusion, my high regard for well-educated persons, my fears and negative opinions about homosexuality, and my trust for an obviously well-meaning and caring therapist, it is not surprising that I easily accepted my therapist's view about my possible lesbianism. By accepting his interpretation I could continue to benefit from and feel the security of that therapy experience; I could latch onto some hope that there was a way out of what I feared was a perverse sexual condition; and I could look forward to the possibility of a more-or-less normal heterosexual life with all the predictability I thought that promised.

AFTER THERAPY:
PICKING UP THE PIECES (1973-1977)

Of course, my experiment in "dealing with my fear of men" did not work, probably because I really wasn't afraid of men–I just wasn't sexually attracted to them. It took the confluence of many elements and events to gradually overcome the homophobic messages of my early development, as well as the impression of a neurotic adjustment that my therapist had left with me. My continuing feelings of attraction toward women would not recede, and demanded that I give consideration to them. I moved away to attend graduate school and developed friendships with new student peers; these new friends did not react in disgust when I confided my struggles about my sexual orientation. A straight feminist therapist helped me understand that lesbianism was an acceptable sexual orientation. The emerging women's movement affirmed the possibilities for women to pursue nontraditional paths. I met lesbians in the university community who did not fit my image of homosexuals as depraved persons, and I actually had a satisfying lesbian relationship while attending graduate school. By the end of my graduate school career I had come to terms with my lesbianism, and had even come out to my family. Although the struggles with nonconscious internalized homophobia continued for many years afterward, I had clearly opened up a new path for myself, and there would be no turning back from the continuing development of a healthy self-image.

I believe I was lucky to have had all these factors come together for me in a relatively brief time. Had I not gone to graduate school and developed supportive friendships, had I not found a feminist therapist, or had the times been different, I might not have become aware of the viability of a lesbian lifestyle. So, for me, the detour in my development was not irreversible, but it certainly was a significant life event, and I have spent time and energy undoing and assessing the aftermath of that first therapy experience.

TAKING STOCK:
MY PROFESSIONAL OUTLOOK

After earning my doctorate I accepted an academic appointment in a psychology department offering a degree in clinical psychology, and in two subsequent academic appointments I have continued to be highly involved in graduate education in clinical psychology. For ten years I also saw clients myself, and worked with many gay and lesbian clients in my practice. So I have been in a position to influence students of clinical psychology, and have also had the responsibility of working with clients addressing sexual orientation issues.

Did my early therapy experience affect how I related to my therapy clients? Most certainly. As clients queried me about my sexual orientation, I was cognizant of their fears that I might either condemn them for being homosexual or confirm their own homophobic feelings. As gay or lesbian clients contemplated ending their heterosexual marriages, I was aware of their torment about whether they could lead a "normal" life *and* have a satisfying relationship. As heterosexual clients recounted distress and confusion over the demise of their marriage to a gay man or lesbian, I understood their sense of futility about saving the marriage, and the fear and shame associated with trying to explain to friends and family why their marriage was dissolving. That is, my experiences allowed me to empathize with the conflicts my clients experienced over sexual orientation issues. But that, I think, was only a small part of the impact of my own therapy experience.

What was perhaps a more significant effect of my therapy experience was my understanding of the power that the therapist has over the client. As I worked with clients who were in distress, I was very aware of how their distress might predispose them to hang on my every word, looking for a way out of their pain. As clients explained their fears about how people in general might react to their sense of differentness, I was aware of how the words of an apparently well educated expert, an expert in psychology no less, would weigh on them. And when clients asked me what they should do about a given problem, I was aware that my words could easily direct them to take a particular action upon leaving my office. I understood that regardless of whether *I* felt powerful, my clients were often imbuing me with power, and that I had a great responsibility as a therapist not to misuse this power.

As an educator, this lesson has influenced me in two ways. First, I know that as an instructor and supervisor I clearly have power over students by virtue of the role I play in evaluating their performance and guiding their education. This position of power also carries with it a responsibility to use this power to foster the student's education and professional development, albeit within the parameters of the educational and professional standards.

Second, I believe it is important to instill in students an understanding of the power differential in the therapy relationship. Many students understand this already, but others are naive about it, or believe that the therapist should certainly use this as well as any other tools available to him/her to influence the client. Students who are naive about the power differential generally come to understand the nature of the therapist's power after some discussion and concrete examples of it (giving examples of the power differential between the instructor-student is one way to help students relate to the therapist-client power differential). But students (and professionals for that matter) who believe that therapists should use their power–because they are the experts and know what is best for the client–are the ones who are most likely to abuse that power. Unfortunately, they are the ones who are least amenable to understanding how power can be abused, and thus present the greatest challenge to the educator. However, given my personal understanding of the great impact a therapist can have on a client, I believe that it is imperative to educate students carefully on this count.

EPILOGUE: POWER AND RESPONSIBILITY

Interestingly, a dozen years after this early therapy experience I had occasion to cross paths with my first therapist. We talked about my experience of the therapy, and I explained how I had felt influenced by him, and had taken a detour in my personal development. He was appropriately embarrassed by this revelation. Apparently, his views on gay/lesbian issues had evolved quite significantly in the intervening years, and I doubt that he was still making the same "mistakes" with current clients. It was nevertheless gratifying to talk to this man, professional to professional, about how he had influenced me. It is my hope that these kinds of discussions can be more commonplace among professionals. It is too easy to lose sight of how much influence we have over clients, and we all must remember the incredible burden of responsibility that our professional role carries.

From the Inside Out

P. Lauren Levy

SUMMARY. The author chronicles her personal experiences as both a client and therapist from her perspective as a lesbian. Using the timeline of her own therapy, she discusses her personal insights as they arose in her therapy; this includes her decision not to marry as well as uncovering memories of incest. She highlights the major influences and events surrounding her decision to become a counselor, and relates her past to the current theoretical framework that she uses in her work. Specifically, she mentions the work of Carl Rogers, the feminist movement, and her current interest in Self Psychology. She discusses her views about sharing personal information with her clients and how it relates to her sexual orientation. *[Article copies available from The Haworth Document Delivery Service: 1-800-342-9678.]*

Looking back on my decision to become a therapist I can see that the seeds were planted early. My life experiences taught me to observe and interpret behavior as a matter of survival.

I entered my first therapy office when I was twenty-one years old because I thought I was going crazy. I had not been sleeping more than a couple of hours a night for the past three months. Sleeping pills and tranquilizers did not help. I was student teaching and engaged to be married. I had minimal insight into my internal pro-

---

P. Lauren Levy, MEd, CADAC, is a counselor in private practice. She lives in Tucson, AZ with her life-partner of twelve years.

[Haworth co-indexing entry note]: "From the Inside Out." Levy, P. Lauren. Co-published simultaneously in *Women & Therapy* (The Haworth Press, Inc.) Vol. 18, No. 2, 1996, pp. 19-23; and: *Lesbian Therapists and Their Therapy: From Both Sides of the Couch* (ed: Nancy D. Davis, Ellen Cole, and Esther D. Rothblum) The Haworth Press, Inc., 1996, pp. 19-23; and: *Lesbian Therapists and Their Therapy: From Both Sides of the Couch* (ed: Nancy D. Davis, Ellen Cole, and Esther D. Rothblum) Harrington Park Press, an imprint of The Haworth Press, Inc., 1996, pp. 19-23. Single or multiple copies of this article are available from The Haworth Document Delivery Service [1-800-342-9678, 9:00 a.m. - 5:00 p.m. (EST)].

19

cess. It was many months before I knew that I needed to end the engagement and many years before I knew that I was a lesbian. Although my therapy lasted only a few months, I view it as crucial to my survival. I was in crisis and those months anchored me in turbulent times. They also provided me with my first female role model who believed in my courage and strength and provided a glimpse of possibilities larger than my own pain.

My therapist leaned toward a Rogerian approach in her therapy. With her gentle encouragement I began reading some of Carl Roger's (1961) writings. I was impressed by his willingness to discuss his internal process in a professional setting. It provided me with insight into an image of an integrated self.

In therapy, I felt safe in an atmosphere of acceptance, patience, and understanding. In retrospect, I remember my therapist asking me about my relationship and if I really wanted to get married. I don't think that I ever really heard those questions; I was not ready. I often remember that when I become impatient and expect clients to change or understand something before they are ready.

It was seven years later that I came out as a lesbian. Although the coming out process was difficult, it did not occur to me to seek therapy. Falling in love had its own therapeutic healing. Claiming my sexuality and my sexual orientation actually relieved much of the internal struggle rather than adding to it; I now had a label to explain why I felt so unsettled. I was lucky to quickly find a supportive community of women and I felt that I had a place where I belonged.

My life at that time was greatly influenced by both the feminist and lesbian movements. I learned that the internalized oppression and self-hate I felt were caused by the larger culture in which I was living. Within that context, I began to design a new image for myself as a woman. Slowly, I began to envision myself as competent, seeing the first glimmer of a future that I could actively create.

This part of my journey took me on a two-and-a-half-year trip through much of North America travelling in a van with my lover. This was an important transition time. With hindsight I understand my need to leave behind my old life, thereby shedding much of the self-limiting expectations imposed on children growing up in the fifties. I was clear that the housewife role would not be an option for me. Seeing the world in a new way allowed me to see my life with new possibilities.

My next encounter with a formalized therapy process was at the breakup of a four year relationship. At that point, finding a therapist who was sensitive to lesbian issues was a priority. After several months, the therapist told me that she was in love with me and could no longer see me in a professional capacity. She said that she would not be able to see me for two years, but broke that pledge and called me within four months saying that she could not stay away from me. I was aware of the power that she had in her role as my therapist, because although I knew that the situation was not right, I still saw her. I am grateful for the strength and clarity that I eventually found to end my contact with her even though she persisted in calling me. This situation could have been even more traumatic had I not been able to end it so quickly. It should not have been my responsibility to end it; it was hers to have not started it.

Based on this experience, I have become acutely aware of the power and responsibilities that are inherent in the therapeutic relationship. I am vitally aware of the importance of maintaining clear boundaries with clients while working to understand the dynamics related to transference and countertransference. While it is not unusual for clients and therapists to share caring feelings about each other, it is important for the therapist to understand her own feelings and to take conscious responsibility for how those feelings are enacted. It is also the responsibility of the therapist to assist the client in understanding their reactions in a supportive and non-shaming environment while clearly defining the parameters of the therapeutic relationship.

Unknown to myself at the time, I began training to become a therapist. I believe that it was partially due to my active interest in women's issues, particularly rape crisis work. I started as a volunteer and have continued to work in the mental health field since that time. I was quickly contracted by that agency to work on a grant for prevention of child sexual abuse. In that role, I wrote and published curricula and developed training for teachers in many of the local school districts. Although I was excited by the work in child sexual abuse, I continued to feel a subtle anxiety around my work. Panic attacks and sleep disturbances reappeared. It took four years of work in that field to begin to allow my own memories of sexual abuse and incest to emerge. Again, I entered therapy, this time for five years.

It is with feelings of relief, compassion and gratitude that I remember those five years. Sometimes it is hard to believe that part of my life is in the past since, for so long, it encompassed most of my life and being. I believe that it is the most courageous work that I have done and perhaps will ever be called upon to do. Because of my own experiences in healing from incest, I also have the utmost confidence in my client's abilities to walk through their pain to attain the healing that they are desperately seeking.

I have been clean and sober from alcohol and drugs for nine years. For seven of those nine years I was actively involved in Twelve Step Programs. I learned a lot from that model of recovery which helped me create a therapeutic milieu for myself. I developed a personal concept of spirituality, a community of support and a way to self-examine my personal involvement in my problems. I have much respect for the teachers and peers whom I have met in those rooms.

For a few years I worked in alcohol and drug treatment. I began to feel hindered by the treatment model and its limitations in working with many of the more complex problems of dual diagnosed clients. It was at that point that I decided to work in private practice, particularly to have the freedom to explore other therapeutic approaches which fit with my own experiences as a client and therapist.

My current approach in therapy continues to evolve. My professional interest is in working with more complex issues that involve longer-term therapy. Based on my own experience as a client and therapist, I believe that fundamental change happens for people in an environment where they feel supported in exploring their own feelings, beliefs and experiences. For many clients, a short-term model, although economically more feasible, may deny the importance of that exploration. As Karen Ahbel (1994) so aptly wrote, "As a psychotherapist, I am concerned about the tension between managed time and the creative relational time that is intrinsic to the psychotherapy process. While we cannot shrink from the question of who will pay for this time, we must speak up for the truth that psychotherapy's time does not easily lend itself to being managed."

Currently I find myself being influenced by the study of Self Psychology. This approach believes that much of human behavior is about the need of the individual to establish an internally integrated sense of self. Helene Jackson (1991) writes that by using this approach change occurs ". . . in the surround of an empathic milieu, fostered by the use of therapeutic interventions of acceptance, understanding and explanation." The therapeutic relationship and the willingness of the therapist to be present in the session are cornerstones in this process.

Being counselors asks much of us. Being a lesbian and a counselor is a challenging balance. Because of the fear and shame that surrounds homosexuality in this culture, some of us may feel a necessity to shield ourselves in secrecy, hiding those parts of ourselves that feel most vital. The decision to share personal information may feel like the same struggle for acceptance as it feeds into our own internalized shame. However, that decision needs to be based on an examination of the effects that sharing personal information have on the therapeutic relationship. I am careful about what I share during a session, not because I am a lesbian, but because as a counselor I am responsible to my clients in their therapeutic process. As a counselor, I ask myself to share my humanness with my clients as they struggle to understand their own. As a lesbian, I must ask myself to understand my lesbianism as a part of my humanness.

For me, part of the excitement of being a counselor is bearing witness to the process of growth and healing. As I write this, I wonder how my life and thoughts will evolve from this point. My hope is that as I reread this in the coming years, I will continue to be awed by the journey of life.

REFERENCES

Ahbel, K. (1994, March/April). Time to wait. *Common Boundary*, pp. 49-52.
Jackson, H. (Ed.). (1991). *Using self psychology in psychotherapy*. Northvale, NJ: Jason Aronson Inc.
Rogers, C. (1961). *On becoming a person*. Boston: Houghton Mifflin Company.

From the Other Side of the Couch: A Lesbian Psychiatrist Looks at Her Own Therapy

Nancy D. Davis

SUMMARY. This article gives an intimate account of the author's own therapy and shows how the effects of white male heterosexual privilege altered the outcome of her own therapy in subtle ways. The article also deals with the boundary violations which occurred in the course of therapy with three different therapists of both sexes. These breaches of good therapeutic practice were influenced by the fact that the author is both a lesbian and a practicing physician. *[Article copies available from The Haworth Document Delivery Service: 1-800-342-9678.]*

INTRODUCTION

My purpose in writing this article is to illustrate with my personal story how far the roots of our patriarchal society invade women's and especially lesbian's lives, and even in the therapy room. The therapy that we lesbians experience is inevitably tainted by white

Nancy D. Davis, MD, is a practicing psychiatrist who began her professional life in internal medicine. After 25 years of healing the body, she became a psychiatrist to heal the psyche. She is a life-long lesbian who has been in a joyous relationship with her partner for 47 years despite the rigors of medical practice.

[Haworth co-indexing entry note]: "From the Other Side of the Couch: A Lesbian Psychiatrist Looks at Her Own Therapy." Davis, Nancy D. Co-published simultaneously in *Women & Therapy* (The Haworth Press, Inc.) Vol. 18, No. 2, 1996, pp. 25-36; and: *Lesbian Therapists and Their Therapy: From Both Sides of the Couch* (ed: Nancy D. Davis, Ellen Cole, and Esther D. Rothblum) The Haworth Press, Inc., 1996, pp. 25-36; and: *Lesbian Therapists and Their Therapy: From Both Sides of the Couch* (ed: Nancy D. Davis, Ellen Cole, and Esther D. Rothblum) Harrington Park Press, an imprint of The Haworth Press, Inc., 1996, pp. 25-36. Single or multiple copies of this article are available from The Haworth Document Delivery Service [1-800-342-9678, 9:00 a.m. - 5:00 p.m. (EST)].

25

male heterosexual privilege. Sexist bias exists in us all, and exists at a subconscious level in all of our therapists. Often it is at a conscious level as well. Unless the patriarchal thinking has been rigorously addressed by our therapists, be they male or female, therapy will be tinted and tainted by this cultural bias. I also wish to address the violations of my boundaries because I see clearly how these violations have been hurtful to me even though they were not as severe as others have experienced. I suffered these violations with therapists of both sexes. My story is offered for the enlightenment of others, so that in the future therapists may, with understanding, avoid some of the pitfalls exemplified in my own therapy.

BEGINNING THERAPY

Although I had experienced feelings of depression, worthlessness, and being unlovable all my life, it never occurred to me that those feelings were either abnormal or remediable. I thought that I was born with personality inadequacies, and that those feelings were a natural consequence of this. I also believed that I was ugly, selfish, lazy, and stupid, because I was told these things by my parents. Although I wasn't told them on a daily basis, it was often enough to have me really believe them on some deep level. As I grew up, I learned to hide some of those feelings from others and certainly from myself. But when my life didn't go well, or, as frequently happened, I became depressed, then I knew for a certainty that my feelings of unworthiness were justified. The pain I experienced at those times I have now learned to call shame (the feeling of being defective or not OK). Surely, it is the most painful of human emotions, and we all will go far to avoid reexperiencing the pain of our childhood shame.

Despite my "laziness" and "stupidity," I did well in school and graduated from high school with honors and two scholarships. These and some emotional and financial support from my grandmother enabled me to go to college. To my amazement, I was not only able to graduate from college but was accepted into medical school. The days in medical school were difficult because I always had the lurking fear that I would ultimately flunk out, and this lasted to the very day of graduation. The climate in my medical school fostered those fears. It also taught the students to build their own self-esteem at the expense of others, by tearing them down, as was done to us. Therefore any showing of weakness, such as expressing feelings, would make one extremely vulnerable.

Later, in internship and a residency in internal medicine, I was terrified that I wouldn't "measure up." Therefore I did what I had always done and worked even harder to try to prove to myself that I was "OK" after all. My achievements did nothing to assuage my basic feelings of worthlessness. My discovery in my sophomore year in college that I was lesbian only reinforced my feelings of being unacceptable. Indeed, in the 1950s homosexuals were unacceptable in "normal" society. Hard work helped to distract me from those awful feelings, but even then my fears of being exposed as a lesbian, and my fears of being inadequate as a practicing physician, kept me from experiencing any satisfaction from my obvious successes.

It was only at the age of 48 that I first considered therapy, and that was after a friend [also a physician] had found some help in his life from a psychiatrist. I knew that my life had been a great struggle and that my life could be happier and easier. The thought that in therapy I would have to expose my homosexuality and my fears about my own inadequacies terrified me. I also had the misguided fear that I would be found to be "too emotionally weak" to be practicing medicine safely. These fears were in spite of the fact that I had always been successful in any professional venture that I undertook. Finally I came to the conclusion that there was no other way for my life to be different and, therefore, I decided to take the risk to see Jim. My previous experience with psychiatrists was limited to those who seemed "bizarre" at best and "unhinged" themselves, at the worst.

In 1976 I began therapy with Jim who, fortunately, was a psychiatrist unlike my negative stereotype. I began therapy while I was a practicing internist and terminated 18 months later, except for a brief period in 1982 during the beginning of my training in psychiatry. I also did individual therapy with Grace, a Ph.D. psychologist, beginning in 1982 and lasting two years. After a year of individual therapy, I started in group therapy with Grace and Tom as co-therapists, and this was of 18 months duration, ending in 1985. I also was in individual therapy with Tom, a psychiatrist, for one year, also ending in 1985, which coincided with the completion of my psychiatric training. This article is written from the vantage point of ten years after completing all formal therapy. Throughout the subsequent years I have continued on a path of personal growth and have made many more gains than I accomplished during formal therapy.

THERAPY WITH JIM

I remember very well my feelings before that first visit to Jim's office. I was filled with dread that my worst fears about myself would be confirmed, and fear that simply going to a psychiatrist would make me seem emotionally unfit to be a physician. I remember nothing of the details of that actual visit, except at the end when I told him that I didn't wish any professional courtesy. Jim replied that he never gave any, and the way he said it felt like a rebuke to me for mentioning it. I must have cringed, because he looked hard at me and said "Were you abused?" I hastily denied it, as "abuse" seemed to be a bad thing, and at that time I didn't know that I was, indeed, abused as a child–emotionally, physically, and sexually. In the 18 months of that first therapy, the subject of abuse was never raised again. I remember that because I feared that the subject might come up again and was relieved that it didn't.

In his waiting room, I was always so filled with anxiety that I could feel my heart pounding. Nothing was explained to me about how therapy worked, how long it took, or what the goals might be, but he did assure me of confidentiality. We sat in chairs opposite each other with two footstools between us. Jim sat with his feet up on his footstool, and there was a prescription pad and a flyswatter beside him on the floor. I know that I had an emotional reaction to the flyswatter at the time, but it was many years later that I recalled that in my family a flyswatter was used to swat kids, in addition to flies.

I believe that I had instant father transference with Jim, and immediately set about trying to get the love and respect from him that I hadn't gotten from my own father. It is unfortunate that this transference wasn't addressed, because it got in my way of my ability to address my feelings. I would just sit and cry about how awful I felt about myself, and of course, I was fearful of being judged as my father had judged me. Finally, Jim got up and approached my chair, and said "I can't let you do that–just cry." I wasn't sure what that meant, but the words felt caring to me, and not angry or critical like my father. I felt less like a specimen, and less judged; and gradually I was able to talk more. I came to trust that Jim meant well, but I wasn't comfortable enough to be honest with him about my deepest fears. I couldn't tell Jim about the despair that I experienced about myself, for fear that he would see me as "weak" and incompetent as a physician.

Gradually I felt comfortable in talking with Jim about my professional fears of not knowing enough and of being a failure. After all, he was physician, too, and could understand what it was like to bear awesome responsibilities. Earlier in my professional life I had given all that I had to my patients until, after several years, I simply burned out. It had happened twice before, and I was approaching it a third time. Jim helped me see that I was "allowed" to take care of myself, too, and then practicing medicine became less of a burden, although still rigorous. He also helped me to look at practical ways that I might make life a little easier for myself.

When it came to my homosexuality, I was ultimately able to talk about it, although I feared that I would be labeled as "pathological." After all, Jim held that the theory of "penis envy" was correct, and that I as a woman had had to deal with the disappointment of having "second class" genitalia. I did get acceptance from Jim about being a lesbian but not the validation I needed to help heal the shame of being homosexual, and a woman, in our homophobic and sexist society. I felt that my status as a physician helped me, in his eyes, to "rise above" the lower status of being a woman, and as lover of women, I was more like a man than a woman.

I did get the validation from Jim that my mother was emotionally abusive. He called her narcissistic, but didn't explain what that was, and I was afraid to ask. Some years later, when I read Alice Miller's *Drama of the Gifted Child* (1981), I came to understand that there was something wrong with my mother's treatment of me, not that I was defective. Strangely, we touched little on my father who was also very abusive to me, especially during my high school years, with his daily "put downs" over matters as small as the order of eating the food on my plate.

Therapy terminated with Jim when he said that he had helped me to deal with my narcissistic mother as much as he could. I felt abandoned by him but he spoke the truth, because he was limited in dealing with his own narcissistic mother. It was his acceptance of his status quo that led me to accept my own, and for me to accept so many more years of abuse from my mother. Jim didn't recognize the difference between the treatment of sons and the treatment of daughters by a narcissistic mother. Sons are seen to be a source of glory for the narcissistic mother, as the world values men and their achievements. Daughters are seen as an extension of the mother, and therefore must present a carbon copy of the mother's perceived inflated image of herself. The daughter has the almost impossible task of fulfilling the mother's expectations of her.

I did begin to see Jim again after starting my psychiatric residency. In the intervening time my internal medical practice had become increasingly psychologically oriented, and I saw that healing with medication was often inadequate to deal with my patients' pain. I saw that healing with psychotherapy was more efficacious and finally, at the age of 52, decided to take the risk of changing my specialty to psychiatry.

Soon after starting my psychiatric residency I became depressed over the inhumane way patients and staff were treated in the mental hospital where I worked. After only several visits Jim became acutely ill with cancer of a variety with an extremely poor prognosis. Despite this he returned to work, and it is amazing that he did so, given his own problems. Again, I could only cry during our sessions. This time I was consciously fixed on his near and inevitable death. As I continued to do nothing but weep during the session, and Jim couldn't seem to help me with my problem with his illness or any other problems, I decided to leave therapy. At this point, he ventured to say that my distress with his illness was probably from transference, but didn't offer to help me work it out. Later, I came to see that Jim was right; my father had died from cancer after a short illness, one week before I graduated from medical school, and I had never really dealt with the grief.

In summing up my therapy with Jim, I must say that the therapy was helpful in many ways, but it was superficial and behaviorally oriented. It didn't address the intense shame I experienced as a result of my childhood of abuse and even failed to address the abuse itself. This meant that I continued to see myself as unalterably flawed. His flagrant violation of my boundaries by involving me in his private life made me angry soon after I left therapy with him, but my anger about the lack of attention to transference issues only came to me much later. His failure to seek help for his personal issues of a failed marriage and life endangering illness, and his following his agenda in therapy rather than mine, prevented me from dealing with my issues. The other aspects of my therapy that were even more detrimental were related to my being a woman and a lesbian. Even in therapy, I wasn't allowed to be the woman that I really was because as a lesbian I was assumed to fit the male inspired stereotype of a "husband."

I think that he couldn't understand what it was like being a woman in a man's world. A physician himself, Jim accepted me as a "brother," and could not see the sexism of the medical fraternity. He didn't see how the sexist approach of my parents caused me such a deep sense of shame for being "less than" my brother. Likewise, he didn't see how our homophobic society increased my burden of shame. Unless one has lived "underground," as an alien in the dominant heterosexual culture, I don't think one can appreciate what it was like for me to be continually hiding, and living in constant fear that discovery of my homosexuality would destroy my personal and professional life. Jim could remarry, and be open about the joy in his new relationship, while that was never an option for me. He didn't understand how I yearned to stop living the heterosexual lie, and to live openly with the woman who has lovingly shared my life for 47 years.

THERAPY WITH GRACE

It was a stormy evening with sheets of rain pouring down when my partner took me to my first visit with Grace. It was several months after my traumatic termination with Jim, and by this time I was in a state of clinical depression. I was feeling beleaguered in the residency program over the fight to keep my sense of values in that place of abuse called a mental health facility. This raised all my issues of core shame which had not been addressed in my therapy with Jim, and therefore did not help me to make real change in the core pain I bore since early childhood. Grace, on the other hand, was able to hear my pain and just listen. It was my agenda and my needs which were paramount, and enabled me to make life changes. With her encouragement I was able to access my deep feelings of fear of my parents. As a small child I feared that they would kill me if I wasn't "good." My fear and shame were so strong that at times I couldn't speak at all. No matter how hard I tried, my tongue wouldn't work. It shocked me to note that when I began to speak of sensitive issues my tongue wouldn't articulate my feelings. It is clear to me that a woman therapist was much safer for me, but at times I feared that even she might be abusive like my mother.

I had the feeling that first night I met with Grace that she was lesbian, too, but didn't bring it up until the end of therapy, when she said that she had had some lesbian relationships but was in doubt as to her sexual orientation. Then I understood my feelings of lack of support from Grace of my being lesbian.

I also felt a lack of support from Grace of my being a woman. I really needed this validation because of my own male chauvinism, learned from the medical community. Later, after my therapy ended, I learned from Grace that she had some gender confusion, arising from the way she was treated by her family.

It was during my therapy that Grace agreed to my request for us to become friends after the therapy was over. It was during my therapy that she involved me in her professional activities. I was gratified by Grace's willingness to be my friend, but was disturbed by the dual relationship in working with her outside of the therapy room.

To sum up my experience with Grace as a therapist, she gave me a safe place in which to explore some of the traumas of my childhood, and wholly supported that endeavor. It helped ameliorate some of the shame. Again, there were boundary violations, and again, the fact that she hadn't come to terms with her own narcissistic mother limited me in doing so. Again, there was not as much validation for my sexual orientation and gender as would have been most helpful, but I could be a woman and be my lesbian self with her. Unlike Jim, she was almost entirely passive as a therapist, offering very few interventions, but was willing to educate me when I requested it. She was also willing to do supervision with me when I got into trouble with my own clients, as I was a student therapist by this time and in need of this help.

GROUP THERAPY

It was no wonder that Tom evoked my transference feelings from my father since he was clearly "papa" to the group. We group members waited to see what he would say before responding to each other, and expected that he would find a solution to any problem presented by group members. Although he was always kindly (unlike my rageful father), he was still the authority. This was like my father, and so many other men with whom I had had contact. Still, we all loved Tom and I was willing to accept his authoritarian ways just as I did with my own father because I didn't know that there was a choice.

I credit group therapy with teaching me that I am lovable. I believe that there is no other way that I could have learned it, as that knowledge came through my relationship with the others in the group. First, I saw that they could accept my homosexuality without turning away; and later, I saw that they came to love me, despite really "knowing" me. I really felt their love for me when I terminated with the group, and they formed a circle around me in sort of a group hug. It was a peak experience which I shall never forget. It helped lift me out of some of that immobilizing shame which I had experienced all my life from my feelings of "defectiveness." This personal experience has influenced my professional life by causing me to start groups to provide the same kinds of experiences.

The salutary effect of my group experience was affected by the fact that Grace and Tom were at odds because he was overly directive in the group and was unable to listen to Grace. In addition, Tom was abusive with his smoking addiction by making us breathe his smoke. Grace essentially withdrew from her co-therapist's role rather than confront Tom.

The other positive experience in group was learning about my father's whipping of my brother and me when we were quite small.

I had repressed my memories of them. These came back to my conscious mind through a tremendous fear response after a group member vented her anger by pounding furiously on the couch pillows. I became panic stricken and tried to leave the room. From this, my memories came flooding back of my father whipping me, and I had a mental picture of myself, as a toddler, on our kitchen floor trying to crawl away from his blows. It was a powerful emotional experience to revisit this scene from my early childhood. I understood then where much of my fear originated.

When I checked out the whippings with my mother, she confirmed that my father made a "cat o' nine tails" from one of his belts for the purpose of whipping us. She thought that my father had whipped me because I was homosexual. How would he have known that when I was so young?

THERAPY WITH TOM

Individual therapy with Tom was suggested to me as an opportunity to deal with the transference issue of seeing older, gray haired men as my critical and abusive father. These transference feelings had come up in group with Tom, and I thought that as a therapist myself I ought to work on my issues with men.

What came out of this part of my therapy surprised me. I came to learn consciously about the sexual abuse at the hands of my mother, and for a long time I hated to be touched by anyone. Tom helped me discover my past so that I could deal with it in the present, and this process has been very helpful to me. Tom insisted that my father's whipping me wasn't very important in my emotional development, because I was able to love my father and even grieve at his untimely death.

CONCLUSIONS

None of the three therapists from whom I sought help was really able to fulfill my needs, but each one helped me, and in a different way. Though a large part of what I learned about myself came from my own efforts, I needed a start from my therapists. I had to learn that there was an inner self which was worthwhile in order to be able to hear its voice, and I couldn't do that until I learned that I wasn't born defective, and wasn't so immobilized by shame. I continued to blame myself for my unhappiness until I understood and experienced the pain of my childhood. Each therapist helped me to see a part of the abuse I suffered as a child at the hands of my narcissistic mother and alcoholic father. I came to see the abuse gradually, as I wouldn't have been able to withstand the pain of all that knowledge at once. I am certain that I needed time to assimilate the pain. Even today, almost 20 years since I first began therapy, I become aware of new evidences of what Alice Miller calls "soul murder." Such knowledge helps me forgive myself for what I am, damaged, but viable as a person. I continually need to remind myself of what it was like for me as a child so that I don't continue to blame myself for my current difficulties.

As I review my experience with the three therapists, I am struck by the boundary invasions of all three: Jim, by the intrusion of his private life into the therapeutic hour; Grace, by allowing the prospect of friendship after the therapy was over, and accepting me as a colleague before I was ready for that; and Tom, by making the group members submit to inhaling his smoke and not even permitting discussion of our feelings when the subject came up.

I also want to comment on the fact that none of my therapists was able to validate me as a lesbian woman, although not one was sexist or homophobic. Growing up in a home which only valued males, and in a society which only valued the white heterosexual male, I had much to overcome to feel accepted by the world. White male privilege is so pervasive in our society that few of us see it unless some circumstance points it up for us. Jim and Tom accepted me into the physician "brotherhood," and as a result, I became one of the "boys." This meant that I had to disavow my femininity in the therapy room, as I had done in the hospital, in order to be accepted by my colleagues. I am not saying that I was pushed into this role with them. I am saying that they took my stance as part of me, and didn't recognize that being "one of the boys" was only protective, and prevented me from being authentic. Neither one could understand what it was like to grow up as a female in this society. Not one validated my lesbian sexual orientation as a legitimate lifestyle and my relationship to be the equal to heterosexual marriage. Grace couldn't help me be a self-respecting woman because she was in doubt about her own femininity. Likewise, she couldn't validate me as a lesbian, because she was uncertain about her own sexual orientation. Jim and Tom didn't really understand that I needed this validation. Though neither one was overtly homophobic, they couldn't understand what it was like to live as a lesbian in the time that I did when most homosexuals were "in the closet." Although these divergences from good therapy practice may seem small in comparison with grosser therapist misconduct, they resulted in significant delays in my recovery.

These are the problems that lesbians and women face at the hands of heterosexual male therapists who may be well meaning but inexperienced. Wherever possible for lesbians, I recommend lesbian therapists who have dealt with their own internalized homophobia; and in cases where a client is having trouble with her identification as a woman, a female therapist who herself has dealt with her internalized male chauvinism.

What also strikes me is that to some degree, I, too, have unintentionally committed boundary invasions with my clients, and they were similar in nature to the ones I had experienced as a client. It seems to me, that as parents teach their children about parenting by their own example, so clients of therapists are taught how to do therapy by example. Over the years, I have often been consciously aware of what I took from Jim, Grace, and Tom. I value them all as "parents" in my personal life, because they helped me to be no longer a victim of my past. I also value them as teachers in my professional life, and unconsciously, as well as consciously, I model my therapeutic behavior after theirs. Some of this is beneficial, but not all. The laxity about client-therapist boundaries is taught in the same way that blurring boundaries between family members is taught by example in dysfunctional families. Therefore, I believe that all therapists have the duty to examine themselves over the issue of maintaining proper boundaries with their clients. I also believe that therapists have the duty to learn about the special needs of their clients and seek appropriate supervision.

REFERENCE

Miller, A. (1981). *The drama of the gifted child.* N.Y.: Basic Books.

From Personal Therapy to Professional Life: Observations of a Jewish, Bisexual Lesbian Therapist and Academic

Sari H. Dworkin

SUMMARY. First, this article describes and critiques two personal therapy experiences where the author's sexual preference and Jewish identities were part of the presenting problems. In the critique of personal therapy the focus is on how the therapists' lack of training about the effects of marginal identities on psychological make-up and functioning was detrimental to healing. Second, the article moves on to an exploration of the author's part-time therapy practice and role as a counselor-educator in academia. The university where she teaches is in a conservative, agricultural area, which often makes the concepts important to the author difficult to convey. Finally, the article concludes with guidelines for therapists. *[Article copies available from The Haworth Document Delivery Service: 1-800-342-9678.]*

INTRODUCTION

I have been in and out of therapy throughout my adult life. The key issues for me should have been my dysfunctional family of

---

Dr. Sari H. Dworkin is Professor of Counseling at California State University-Fresno, and a licensed psychologist and marriage, family and child counselor in part-time, private practice. She received her PhD degree from the University of Nebraska-Lincoln.

[Haworth co-indexing entry note]: "From Personal Therapy to Professional Life: Observations of a Jewish, Bisexual Lesbian Therapist and Academic." Dworkin, Sari H. Co-published simultaneously in *Women & Therapy* (The Haworth Press, Inc.) Vol. 18, No. 2, 1996, pp. 37-46; and: *Lesbian Therapists and Their Therapy: From Both Sides of the Couch* (ed: Nancy D. Davis, Ellen Cole, and Esther D. Rothblum) The Haworth Press, Inc., 1996, pp. 37-46; and: *Lesbian Therapists and Their Therapy: From Both Sides of the Couch* (ed: Nancy D. Davis, Ellen Cole, and Esther D. Rothblum) Harrington Park Press, an imprint of The Haworth Press, Inc., 1996, pp. 37-46. Single or multiple copies of this article are available from The Haworth Document Delivery Service [1-800-342-9678, 9:00 a.m. - 5:00 p.m. (EST)].

37

origin and sexual identity confusion, but I wasn't ready to deal with these issues until I was in my late thirties and early forties and none of my therapists confronted my defense mechanism of denial. In critiquing my own therapy I question the lack of confrontation from my therapists. I have never presented as fragile and even though I have been well defended I believe that I have always had enough ego strength and rapport with my therapists that gentle, tentative confrontations would have speeded up my process. Once through the increased anxiety and depression resulting from the confrontations, my subsequent relationships might have been more genuine.

In this article I will concentrate on two therapeutic experiences, one during my doctoral program and one occurring in recent years. Both therapeutic relationships came about as a result of the break-up of an intimate relationship. The first therapy was through a university counseling center with a therapist just completing the psychologist licensing process and occurred when my marriage (to a man) broke up; and the second therapy experience was with a licensed psychologist in private practice and occurred when a relationship with a woman broke up. Both therapists were female, white, non-Jewish and heterosexual. Fictional names and changed descriptions will be used to protect the confidentiality of everyone I describe. First I will discuss and critique my therapy experiences, then I will explore my own practice as a licensed psychologist and licensed marriage, family, and child counselor in private practice, third, my experience as a counselor-educator in a master's degree program, and finally I will end with some guidelines.

CHOOSING A THERAPIST

Nowadays, many people have become better informed consumers of therapy. I often hear lesbians at parties discussing their therapists, experiences in therapy, and how they went about choosing their current therapists. In my clinical courses we explore what clients need to know in order to make an informed decision about therapy.

The first time I chose a therapist it was at the recommendation of women at the university Women's Resource Center. I could only afford to use the free counseling center provided by the university.

No one knew of any lesbian therapists at the counseling center but the therapist recommended to me was known to be a feminist. Leslie was in her early thirties and currently going through the licensing process. She never went over confidentiality, her theoretical orientation, any explanation of the therapy process or gave me any other information necessary for informed consent. We immediately began with why I came to therapy.

A few years ago when I decided I needed therapy, again for financial reasons, I was faced with choosing a therapist from a limited number of therapists who were providers for my insurance company. None of the therapists listed were openly lesbian, which would have been my first choice. A dilemma I would have encountered, if there were any openly lesbian therapists listed, is that because I live in a small community, am a therapist myself, and am a lesbian activist, the possibility of a dual relationship would have presented itself. My next choice for a therapist was to choose a female Jewish therapist. There was one female Jewish therapist on the list and I knew her socially. I chose Joanne because she was female, came recommended by friends, and was believed to be feminist.

My second therapeutic experience with Joanne began with more necessary information than I had been given at the beginning of my first therapy. She did explain confidentiality to me and told me that her theoretical orientation was psychodynamic. At the end of the first session she also informed me that this looked like we were dealing with long-term issues and when the sessions approved by my insurance company ran out, we would discuss how to continue.

THE THERAPEUTIC PROCESS

First Therapy Experience

Leslie was easy to talk to, dressed casually and used a modified Rogerian approach. (By modified I mean that she was more active than Rogerian therapists usually are.) Therapy consisted of clarifying my reasons for leaving my husband and helping me through the grief process. When it came to identity issues, Leslie was less effective as a therapist (although I didn't recognize this at that time). It is important to realize that I had just begun my counseling psychology doctoral program. I was not sophisticated enough about the ingredients of therapy or the implications of identity issues both in terms of my Jewish identity or (at that time) my lesbian identity to know if Leslie was on target.

Raised as a Conservative Jew, one characteristic which attracted me to my ex-husband was his religious observance and his ties to the Jewish community. The Jewish community where we lived was a small community and as far as I was aware, was a heterosexual community. My therapist never explored the importance of Judaism for me and how this loss should have been part of my grief process. My therapist ignored this aspect of my life even though I brought up my Judaism as I invariably do at some point in any close relationship I establish. Perhaps she believed that Judaism wasn't relevant to my therapy as a result of never having explored Judaism as a multicultural issue within her training program. Most therapists, having been raised and socialized in a Christian world, do not realize the impact growing up as a Jew in this society has on the individual (Dworkin, in press). Combine a marginal identity, a Jew, with the marginal identity of a lesbian and these factors become crucial pieces of the psychological make-up of the client (Dworkin, in press).

Leslie ignored my Jewish identity and only minimally assisted in my exploration of my lesbian identity. I was obviously confused, having just ended a heterosexual marriage, moved into an apartment above a house of two lesbian friends, and been thrust into the middle of a lesbian separatist community. Things were happening fast. I already publicly identified as a lesbian but privately, I wasn't sure. Leslie listened empathically and I felt genuine acceptance from her of my newly discovered lesbian preference. Empathic, reflective listening and genuine acceptance by her certainly helped solidify my acceptance of myself as a lesbian but I could have benefited from more. A description of the coming out process (Cass, 1979, Sophie, 1987; Troiden, 1989) would have provided a framework for what I was experiencing and still might experience. Recommendation of reading materials and perhaps a referral to a gay/lesbian affirmative Rabbi would have been helpful. To her credit, Leslie did explore with me the risks and benefits of coming out to various people (family, friends, students, faculty). Leslie was there for me and celebrated my successful coming out experiences and helped me grieve the coming out experiences which led to loss.

While not perfect, therapy with Leslie met most of my needs at that time of my life. Her knowledge of feminism came through when she made interpretations regarding my failed marriage. It was also obvious that feminism helped her to understand and accept my attractions to, love of, and need for closeness with women. Lesbian separatism was new to her but she was able to understand both my need for this philosophy at this time and my confusion about it. (I eventually rejected lesbian separatism as a philosophy that just didn't work for me.) If I could give Leslie advice I would tell her to get more training around lesbian issues and Jewish issues. Perhaps by now she has done this.

The second therapy experience I want to explore was both similar to and different from the experience with Leslie.

Second Therapy Experience

Joanne was a middle-aged, attractive, well-dressed, psychodynamic psychologist. Her manner of dress and her office furnishings suggested affluence. Concentrated eye contact, minimal direction, and well-placed interpretations were the mainstay of her style of therapy. I came to therapy with four issues: the break-up of a relationship with a woman whom I described as having provided me with the best relationship I had had until that point in time, a desire to explore my dysfunctional childhood and my repression of feelings as a result of that childhood, my workaholism, and once again, confusion about my sexual preference.

Joanne let me begin where I wanted to. I chose the break-up of my relationship, an emotional but safer topic than the others. Actually, all of the issues came up because I rambled and jumped from one topic to another. My therapist believed, as she once stated, that the psyche will bring up whatever is necessary. Sometimes I avoided what was scary and she never confronted or interpreted that (at least to me).

The difficulties in my relationship which led to the break-up included an inability for my partner to be there through my emotional struggles. (Dealing with family of origin issues began as a personal exploration before I entered therapy.) My therapist helped me to understand that this relationship was a replica of the relationship I had with my mother. My mother was unable to be emotionally available to me as I was growing up. Another problem with that lesbian relationship was her (she was not Jewish) inability to understand my turmoil about living as a Jew in a Christian society, living as a lesbian Jew in a small Jewish community and almost non-existent lesbian Jewish community. Joanne had more difficulty with this as her training had not explored Jewish issues and it didn't appear to be something around which she had done any personal work.

My stress level was causing me to move back and forth through the stages of the coming out process (Bridgewater, 1992). To add to my confusion, I was beginning to come out as a bisexual after having lived many years solidly committed to a lesbian identity.

Joanne, who rarely asked questions, began to question me about Jewish concerns, the coming out process as a lesbian and as a bisexual (I was able to help with the lesbian identity process, but little was available about bisexuality), and other questions focusing on what it's like to be a non-heterosexual in a heterosexual world. It was obvious to me that many of these questions were for her information and education. I became angry and confronted her about this. Joanne told me that she had never had any training about gay, lesbian, and bisexual issues, and while she had Jewish friends she had never thought about what it was like to be a Jew and especially a Jewish lesbian or bisexual within our culture. My need to educate my therapist interfered with my process; interfered with my rapport with my therapist, my working through of feelings, and my trust in her ability to help me. When I felt that we had gone as far as possible in the exploration of my dysfunctional childhood and how this related to my workaholism, I terminated therapy.

Joanne helped me a great deal. For the first time in my life I didn't need to present myself as perfect without any problems. My feelings were shared with those I trusted and I was able to ask for assistance when needed. I began to say "no" at work and within the community. I was secure in my decision to end my relationship, able to grieve that ending, and able to develop a friendship with my former lover.

Conflicts over my Jewish identity (how to meet these needs) and confusion about my bisexual identity were areas I decided I would have to work on myself. My own therapy practice and academic career helped me in the area of bisexuality and the seeking out of conferences helped me express the pain and develop the support I needed around Jewish non-heterosexual issues.

PROFESSIONAL LIFE

Private Practice

My professional career has been devoted to the study of and the teaching of how to counsel non-heterosexual clients and the teaching of the theory and practice of feminist therapy. When I decided to open a part-time practice to supplement my academic career I purposely advertised as specializing in feminist therapy and sexual orientation issues. To my knowledge I am the only therapist in my community who advertises this way.

My clientele consists primarily of gay, lesbian, and bisexual clients, although I also see heterosexual clients, primarily women seeking independence from traditional roles. Most of my non-heterosexual clients chose me from advertisements within the gay and lesbian community and assume that I am lesbian. I often come out as a bisexual lesbian when I believe it is therapeutically beneficial to the client (as a role model, to illustrate the working through of identity issues).

Recently I have experienced an increase in middle-aged female clients who have been heterosexual all of their lives but now find themselves in love with a woman. These clients do not reconstruct their pasts to conform with their current lesbian lifestyle. They are identifying themselves as bisexual. The exploration my clients are doing in terms of their own sexual identity often matches the personal exploration I have been doing for the past several years (although I come to this exploration from a lesbian rather than heterosexual background). It has also stimulated my current research direction.

Research and practice always involve voluminous reading. In

working with these bisexual women I have seen an acceptance of fluidity of sexual preference (Weinberg, Williams & Pryor, 1994; Weise, 1992), pain over the lack of acceptance of a bisexual identity in the lesbian community (Weinberg et al., 1994; Weise, 1992), and the lack of certainty about their identity which Weinberg et al. (1994) noticed as a difference in the coming out process of bisexuals as compared to gays and lesbians. Weinberg et al. (1994) also found that a majority of those who identified as bisexual in their study came to that identity when they added same-sex experiences or a same-sex partner to a previously heterosexual lifestyle. I have recommended two books on bisexuality which my clients have found helpful: *Closer to Home: Bisexuality & Feminism* (Weise, 1992), and *Bi Any Other Name: Bisexual People Speak Out* (Hutchins & Kaahumanu, 1991). (My clients seem to discover and read books about gay and lesbian lifestyles on their own but have difficulty locating books about bisexuality.)

The theoretical framework which has worked best for me with my clients has been a combination of Self Psychology and Feminist Therapy. I value Self Psychology because the empathic investigation requires understanding the meaning symptoms have in the client's life, and the fostering of mirroring and twinship self-object functions give the client the acceptance she is unable to get elsewhere or give to herself. (For further information about this see Jackson, 1991.) Equally, I value Feminist Psychology because of the acceptance of diversity, the understanding of gender dynamics, and the empowering of women (see Mirkin, 1994).

Translating my beliefs about therapy and working with non-heterosexual clients into a master's level training program hasn't been easy.

Academia

My first task as an academic was to come out so that I could more easily serve as a role model on campus (see Dworkin, 1993). Then I was able to push for coursework on gay, lesbian, and bisexual affirmative counseling and an infusion of these ideas through the curriculum of a master's degree program in marriage, family, and child counseling. In my courses I also explore other issues of identity such as being female in a sexist society and being Jewish in a Christian society.

In order to understand the difficulties I have had it is necessary to note that I work in a conservative, agricultural area. Many of my students come from fundamentalist Christian backgrounds. When they take my courses (and I seem to attract the more open and accepting of these students) they have difficulty integrating what I say with their religious and conservative beliefs. Some of them are able to work through their religious conflicts and feel that they can counsel gay, lesbian, and bisexual clients and other marginalized populations; others realize that they must refer (and we role play ways to do this without being rejecting).

While I feel confident that the students who come through my classes are getting more than the cursory overview one course in multicultural counseling can provide, I am not so confident about other students. These are the people who become the counselors in our community.

For those who understand the ethical duty to refer when they are unable to work with particular clients (and we hope that all of our graduates understand this) there are not many counselors to refer to. I am afraid that many non-heterosexual clients and clients from other marginalized groups in my community have frustrating counseling experiences similar to the ones that I have described.

GUIDELINES AND CONCLUSION

Obviously training, continuing education, and reading are necessary for any therapist to be able to provide the best therapy possible. I believe that multicultural and identity issues must be infused throughout the curriculum. All therapists must personally explore what it is like to be both an oppressor and a member of an oppressed group within our society. While we therapists often rely on our clients to tell us what life is like for them, it is unfair of us to expect our clients to educate us about specific processes such as identity formation and "coming out."

Finally I feel that it is important for therapists to truly be a part of the community they live in. What I mean by that is: get out and meet the various groups and learn about the cultures that make up the community. Most multicultural counseling classes focus on specific populations and omit other populations which may have relevance for the therapist. There are other ways to learn about these populations and therapists must find these other ways. Otherwise we are not truly living up to the ethical principles of "Do good," and "Do no harm."

REFERENCES

Bridgewater, D. (1992). A gay male survivor of antigay violence. In S. H. Dworkin & F. J. Gutierrez (Eds.). *Counseling gay men and lesbians: Journey to the end of the rainbow* (pp. 219-230). Alexandria, VA: AACD Press.

Cass, V. (1979). Homosexual identity formation: A theoretical model. *Journal of Homosexuality, 4*, 219-235.

Dworkin, S. D. (in press). Lesbian and Jewish: Implications for therapy. B. Greene & G. Herek (Eds.). *Lesbian and gay psychology: Ethnic and cultural diversity in the lesbian and gay community.* N.Y.: Sage Publications.

Dworkin, S. H. (1993). Coming out as a lesbian in academia: One woman's experience. In J. T. Gonzalez-Calvo (Ed.). *Gender: Multicultural perspectives* (pp. 289-296). Dubuque, IA: Kendall/Hunt.

Hutchins, L. & Kaahumanu, L. (1991). *Bi any other name: Bisexual people speak out.* Boston: Alyson Publications, Inc.

Jackson, H. (1991). *Using self psychology in psychotherapy.* NJ: Jason Aronson Inc.

Mirkin, M. P. (1994). *Women in context: Toward a feminist reconstruction of psychotherapy.* N.Y.: The Guilford Press.

Sophie, J. (1987). Internalized homophobia and lesbian identity. *Journal of Homosexuality, 14*, 53-65.

Troiden, R. R. (1989). The formation of homosexual identities. *Journal of Homosexuality, 17*, 43-71.

Weinberg, M. S., Williams, C. J. & Pryor, D. W. (1994). *Dual attraction: Understanding bisexuality.* N.Y.: Oxford University Press.

Weise, E. R. (1992). *Closer to home: Bisexuality & feminism.* Seattle, WA: Seal Press.

Reflections of a Midlife Lesbian Feminist Therapist

Elaine Leeder

SUMMARY. In this paper the author evaluates her own work as a lesbian feminist psychotherapist from a critical perspective. Using the work of Kitzinger and Perkins, Carter Heyward and Samuel Sandweiss, she suggests that psychotherapy, as constructed today, has become primarily behavioral, cognitive, apolitical, and disconnected from its original purposes. After describing her own midlife spiritual crisis she details, through journal entries, a journey toward a deeper and more absorbed state of mental health. The author then questions how a therapist might utilize techniques drawn from spiritual and body work practices that might help a client find a place inside that is more soul healing, rather than just of the mind. *[Article copies available from The Haworth Document Delivery Service: 1-800-342-9678.]*

INTRODUCTION

I have been a practicing therapist for the last 25 years. Since the early 1980s I have also identified as a feminist therapist and have

Elaine Leeder, MSW, CSW, MPH, PhD, is Associate Professor and Chair of the Sociology Department at Ithaca College where she also coordinates the Social Work Program. She has written *The Gentle General: Rose Pesotta, Anarchist and Labor Organizer*, State University of New York Press, 1993; and *Treating Abuse in Families: A Feminist and Community Approach*, Springer Publishing Company, 1994.

[Haworth co-indexing entry note]: "Reflections of a Midlife Lesbian Feminist Therapist." Leeder, Elaine. Co-published simultaneously in *Women & Therapy* (The Haworth Press, Inc.) Vol. 18, No. 2, 1996, pp. 47-60; and: *Lesbian Therapists and Their Therapy: From Both Sides of the Couch* (ed: Nancy D. Davis, Ellen Cole, and Esther D. Rothblum) The Haworth Press, Inc., 1996, pp. 47-60; and: *Lesbian Therapists and Their Therapy: From Both Sides of the Couch* (ed: Nancy D. Davis, Ellen Cole, and Esther D. Rothblum) Harrington Park Press, an imprint of The Haworth Press, Inc., 1996, pp. 47-60. Single or multiple copies of this article are available from The Haworth Document Delivery Service [1-800-342-9678, 9:00 a.m. - 5:00 p.m. (EST)].

practiced what I consider to be ethical and political psychotherapy. In addition, I teach and write in the areas of feminism, therapy and international women's concerns. In all my years of practice I have also been in and out of therapy to work on my own issues. In the course of my own personal work I have experienced couples counseling, group therapy, work on eating disorders, individual psychotherapy, and various models of growth-oriented therapy. My therapy helped me to deal with being married, coming out, the breakup of two long-term relationships and other very painful and deep intrapsychic issues. Most of that time I thought that I was getting help as well as helping countless clients who came my way.

Now at the age of 50 I have come to evaluate my therapy, as a therapist and as a recipient of care, in a different and more critical manner. I see that most of that work, be it with psychologists, social workers, or psychiatrists, tends to be behavioral and cognitively directed. I find that this orientation no longer works for me. In fact, I might say, that it really probably never did work. I changed during the course of therapy as much as a result of time and situational changes as the result of therapy. I believe that this can also be said of the work I did with clients.

Recently there has been a spate of books published critiquing the current state of feminist therapy. Books like Kitzinger and Perkins' *Changing Our Minds: Lesbian Feminism and Psychology* (1993) and Carter Heyward's *When Boundaries Betray Us: Beyond Illusions of What Is Ethical in Therapy and Life* (1993) all call into question the nature of feminist therapy today. I find that I am asking myself similar questions, ones which I would like to explore in this paper. These books argue that feminist therapy has lost its political and ethical roots and that for lesbians seeking personal and social change, we are in fact doing a disservice. I would go further and argue that we might also have lost our sense of connectedness with each other and that there is a lack of connection to the deeper and more spiritual aspects of working with people. This connectedness is far more absorbing than is the cognitive or behavioral form of therapy that most of us have had the experience of practicing.

CURRENT CRITIQUE OF FEMINIST THERAPY

Celia Kitzinger and Rachel Perkins (1993) are stirring up quite a controversy with the publication of the book *Changing Our Minds*. In that most provocative book they argue that feminist therapy has become apolitical and has lost its roots. Instead, feminists who were once quite critical of psychology have now given up their skepticism and have substituted "personal explanations for political ones." They have disguised "real material oppression as emotional disturbance." What was once a rebellious language of lesbian feminism has been coopted by the profession of psychology. Words like "power," "freedom," and "liberation" once had meanings that went beyond the individual. Now they are individualistic. They are about freeing the inner child, feeling empowered in one's own life, liberating oneself from bad relationships or seeing the pathology of one's family of origin. Whatever happened to real liberation, power and freedom?, they ask. To them lesbian therapy has become a tool of victimization and "cooling out" of political action.

They also argue that lesbian therapy has undermined the nature of lesbian friendship and community. Once we turned to our sisters, our friends. We built networks that supported us in our pain and sought to create alternative communities, to counter the dominant social forces. Now we seek the therapist to clean up our lives and, in turn, therapy pathologizes us. What were once normal life occurances, breakups, sadness, feeling badly, are now unhealthy. In fact, they argue, it is hard for lesbians to remember that unhappiness is a normal part of life.

Carter Heyward's book *When Boundaries Betray Us: Beyond Illusions of What Is Ethical in Therapy and in Life* (1993) criticizes feminist therapy from the position of that of a client who wants the nature of feminist therapy to change. She believes that therapy is inherently good but is too rigid and boundaried. In a description of her own therapy she had not been able to maintain "empathic connectedness" with her therapist and she felt abandoned and betrayed. She believed that successful therapy would not be too rigid in its imposition of limit setting and that a healthy therapy relationship would allow for intimacy and an authentic emotional connection.

I mention these two books because they are currently being debated in feminist therapy circles and they provide a springboard for me to articulate the arguments that I now have with the very nature of feminist therapy, particularly therapy with lesbians as it has come to be practiced today.

There is also the work of Dr. Samuel Sandweiss which I think is also relevant to my own personal critique of therapy. Dr. Sandweiss is a psychiatrist who began looking at transpersonal psychology in the 1970s. Now, having taken over 17 trips to India to study with his guru Sai Baba, Dr. Sandweiss suggests that western psychology is devoid of any of the elements necessary to bring about true healing in a patient. He argues that there is an extensive amount of work already done on synthesizing psychology and spirituality but that it has never really been seriously integrated into mainstream psychology. He looks to the work of Ernest Becker, Soren Kierkegaard, Arthur Maslow, Otto Rank and Carl Jung for inspiration about the higher states of consciousness, but laments that psychology fails to understand the relationship of higher states of consciousness with the "normal" and "abnormal" mental states with which the field deals.

The work of these authors fairly clearly delineates where I am coming from today. I will tell you the story of my own personal journey, one that began in the summer of 1994, although I now see that it actually began thirty years ago when I rejected organized religion and then became a political activist, atheist, feminist and then lesbian.

MY JOURNEY

In the summer of 1994 I became 50, began menopause, ended a relationship that I had hoped would become a major one in my life and verged on the edge of the worst personal crisis I had had in many years. My friends and I feared for me, so much so that I actually went on medication for awhile, only to develop an agitated depression that was far worse than the original symptoms of sleep problems, suicidal ideation, weight loss and complete despair. I gave up hope. I had done all that I was supposed to do in life. I had two masters degrees and a PhD. I had two published books and countless articles. I had married, had a wonderful child who was now grown, and I had become a lesbian and had been happily partnered for nine years, until six years ago when my lover left for a client of mine. After that I had experienced dating, being involved with wonderful women and I had traveled extensively. I had gone to Africa, and gone around the world teaching on a ship. I had driven myself cross country, and I had been offered a Fulbright. I owned my own home, I had tenure, and I was chair of my department. I was a valued and trusted colleague. I had dear and wonderful friends, at home and in the world. What more did I want? I had it all.

What I realized in all that pain was that I had had an outer life but what was missing was an inner one. All my life I had felt like a shell of a person. I just filled up my emptiness with experiences, people, degrees and eventually I would feel whole, I thought. Well, it did not work anymore. All those coping skills I had developed no longer worked. I was having a midlife crisis and I saw that it was futile.

Into that abyss a friend's hand came. She told me that I was having a spiritual crisis and she offered to do a healing for me. This friend was a healer who I had scornfully derided for months because she was too "new age." I had insulted her and been amused in my political haughtiness at all her "airy fairy" language and images. But I was in so much pain I grudgingly agreed. The first healing, in which I sat leaned against her, felt warm and loving. I had images of my parents come to me, but nothing I had not experienced before. I felt better and the horrible pain in my chest went away for a day, only to return the next. She then suggested that she knew an excellent breathing healer, who could help me. I was cynical but still in pain. I would try anything, just help me want to get up in the morning and take away the ache in my heart and the gagging in my throat.

I actually thought of going to therapy again and, in fact, had one session with my old therapist, who provided me with charts and diagrams "explaining my pain" and from whence it came. The session did nothing for me and I went away 75 dollars poorer and still aching miserably.

I entered the small office and knew immediately I had come to the right place. The waiting room was decorated with African artifacts and collectibles. Six years ago I had gone to Africa after another crisis and had been told there to "go home and heal yourself." I thought I had done that, but clearly my Africa connection was continuing and there was more work to be done.

A tall, white haired and elegant black man greeted me and took me to a small room where he explained to me what was to occur. He then had me lay on a mat on the floor and began to play the most amazing synthesizer music I have ever heard. He taught me how to breathe through my mouth and out my nose and then guided me through a meditation, using the breathing, the music and his voice. Within minutes I was transmuted! I was taken to places I had never been before. There were visualizations, chants, breathing and images that came forth. He worked me through the chakras and helped me to see and feel the pain within my body. In two hours I cried, quaked and then returned, feeling whole and without pain. I knew that I had to return, to do more of this deep and meaningful work.

A few days later I went back for my second session and the work went deeper and I felt even more hopeful. In that session I realized how I had never felt loved nor did I love myself. I worked on letting go of the people who had to leave me and I finally got to my "core." I entered a place I had never reached in psychotherapy. I entered my own soul and felt it deeply. I felt a vibration in my body that actually scared me, but I went with it. My body vibrated so frantically that I was afraid I was hyperventilating. My guide soothed my fear and I went deeper. Finally I saw a white light shining through my body and I began to heal. I could not believe what had happened to me. The radical, feminist, atheist, therapist had had a spiritual experience. It was real, no denying what had happened to me. I left the session still vibrating and it took hours for me to return to my normal state, but now without the chest pain, the gagging and the torment.

I went home after that session, committed to finding other ways of continuing this kind of journey. I knew that psychotherapy, with its behavioral and cognitive approach, did not reach where I needed to go. I wasn't sure how, but I would find a way to experience my self more deeply and to the core I now had an image of.

A few weeks later I called a colleague at work who had been recommended to me for more healing. She taught religious studies at my college and had opened a meditational retreat center not far from home. I had two sessions with her, in which she did energy work healings. She laid me on a table and worked with the energy flow around me. In the first session my dead parents came to me and told me for the first time that they truly loved me and they brought with them the recently deceased Rebbe Schneerson of the Hasidic order of Judaism. My family name had been Sneierson, of that lineage and heritage. I had long ago rejected all of that, but now with my move toward spirituality it was appropriate that my orthodox family background would return and offer me a path.

In the next session a most wonderful event occurred. The pain in my throat had returned and I still felt somewhat tight in the chest. With more energy work my guide was able to help me move the pain right up to my mouth. I began to gag and cough and gag more. I felt like I was in labor somehow and then all at once I spewed forth something. I was not sure what it was, but my guide said that it was a demon. I called it my "dybbuk," a Yiddish word for devil or demon. Alice moved it out of the room and I began to cry hysterically. After I calmed down we both knew something quite meaningful had happened. I had spewed forth a demon from long ago in my life. At that point I knew that I was ready for even more work, work on my soul, on my spirit, on my deepest self.

THE RETREAT

Alice then suggested that I was ready for a three-day silent meditational retreat on the mountain top of her center. I was apprehensive but I trusted that this guide would offer me what I needed. I felt that she was a messenger for me and that I had to listen to her. I did gird myself, however, once again bringing the *New York Times* and books, just in case I could not handle three days of silence, alone.

The following paragraphs are excerpts from the diary I kept those three days. The journal was the only dialogue that I engaged in, alone on that mountain top, surrounded by birds, gurgling brook, deer, late summer fields and a pond. Alice came to me for a few minutes in the morning and at night; she brought food and practices for me to try. Otherwise I was there, by myself, going inward as far as I could go. It was there that I was reborn, at 50, finally becoming a whole person.

8/19/94

Sitting on the deck of my mountain cottage on the first morning of my silent retreat. It has been lovely so far. Alice left me with three things to do: read a few stories about the destruction of the old and going down into the underworld, giving up of the self and dying–metaphorically. I then did a ritual in the moonlight listing all the things I want to let go of and then I burned them while listening to quiet meditational music. It was really quite moving, as I gave up my clutchiness, my fears, anxieties and desperation. The moon was full, the crickets were chirping, the gorge running full with the rain run-off. I wept as I chanted, "my mother, my heart." I am in a crisis of the soul, a dark night of the spirit and this finally feels like the right way to be dealing with it. Drugs and psychotherapy are not the answer anymore.

LATER: Feeling joy! In the sun, on the deck, listening to wonderful music after a morning of spiritual practice, walking in the woods and being with myself as I never have before. I have been visualizing the chakras, saying goodbye and forgiving those who have left me, and forgiving myself for my own flaws and frailties. Each piece builds on the next, helping me to see the terrains of my life with its oceans, deserts and mountains, all to be dealt with as they come my way. I am happy to be here, glad to be on a new journey of self discovery, glad to know a new part of me–a spiritual self that I never knew was within me. I felt joy at the pond, laying in the clover, listening to the stream. This morning I felt thrilled and awed by the butterfly that lighted on my arm and stayed with me for over an hour. I felt glad for the bird feathers I found and I felt so pleased, once again, to be alive. I have found that elusive self deep within. I am glad for the music playing, for the rushing brook, for the smell of my sweating body, for the flowers around me, for my child, for my friends, my home, my job, my ability to find this calm place within. I have been here before, but fleetingly: sitting by the ocean, in the arms of a lover, swimming, writing. But rarely can I get there for any length of time.

Now I know how to do it. I will return to this safe, absorbed place deep within me, again and again, now that I have found it. I have never reached this level of happiness, either through therapy or through relationship. This self is now me, deep and lasting. It resides in my chest, a great white light shines over me and surrounds me. I know it sounds silly, but all these things have happened to me in just this one day.

LATER STILL: Now I am to have a dialogue with my divine friend within. The self who has been with me since birth and the only one to walk with me to death. This self knows all about me, all that I know, feel and have gone through. This divine friend is here with me at all times, even when I forget. When I forget I get lonely and it is a reminder to find that friend within again. The loss of that friend leads to that awful existential angst I always experience—the awareness of the ego. When I find that friend I see that she can be loving and can hold me when I need holding. She can love me unconditionally, as I have never been loved before. That divine friend is my lifelong companion. Even when I condemn her, turn my back on her, am mean to her, she puts up with me the way no one else would. She sees me dissipate myself on relationships, run in fear away from myself, she sees me expend lots of money and energy in ways that do not bring the return I deserve. This divine friend says to me: I love you, Elaine, all that you are within and all that you are without, I love you as you are, you need not change a thing, you are whole as you are, you are lovely, kind, and all that I could need in a friend. This divine friend asks me to take better care of myself; to eat well, exercise and choose how I spend my time wisely. Choose your lovers more carefully, she says, and this divine friend asks and entreats me to love myself as she does. She weeps for the pain I have suffered, laughs for the joy I have known and knows that I am loveable, in the way I do not know myself. This divine friend tells me that I can find her whenever I take a breath, this divine friend is always here with me. All I need is to go inward and there she is; for this divine friend is me.

STILL EVEN LATER: Now I must confront my fears and imagine what I am without them, without my body, without my emotions, without my thoughts, without my work, without my personality, without my consciousness. This will be difficult but try I will:

Who am I without my body? I FEAR I am nothing. Without my

body can I exist or is there something beyond this? If I don't believe there is something called energy then I will live in terror. I remember when my mother died there were ways that she came to me many times, long after her death. She has no body but she is still present, often living in my memory, being called forth in my mind's eye. She exists without a body and so would I without mine.

Who am I without my emotions? My emotions often rule me, they tend to determine how I am in the world. Without them perhaps I would be less colorful, interesting and textured as a person. Without them I would be like all the boring people in the world I never wanted to be like. But without them I might still be me, just less pained.

Who am I without my thoughts? This is hard because my thoughts make me an intelligent being and they have helped me develop a whole life and even a career out of them. But they rule me and my emotions. My thoughts become like a trap, they keep me jailed. I remember reading that "the self emerges between two thoughts" and I am trying now to stay between the thoughts so that the self can come forth. This is the state that I am seeking. I prefer this thought-free state, then I just am, existing, breathing, being. To exist in the world empty of thoughts, that would be bliss.

Who am I without my relationships? At one time I thought I was nothing without them, a lá the Stone Center thinking about women's identity. To be without a primary relationship meant that I did not exist. Now I know that a primary relationship and friendships are important, they do give meaning. But without them I would function, a bit emptier, but still alive. Without relationships I am still me, nonetheless.

Who am I without my work? This is far harder because with no other self definition, at least I have been able to sustain my life through being a therapist, then a professor and now a writer, too. Without my work I feel terror! Without my work there is dead time, nothing to occupy me, no way to prove any meaning to my life. Freud said there is love and there is work. If I have neither can I exist? I think the answer someday will be yes, but for now I must have my work to do service to others. I must work, once again to do work at giving to the world. The answer is that somehow I must keep work as part of my life, for otherwise there is no reason for living. I love to work and will for as long as I am able.

Who am I without my personality? I would be boring. It defines who I am, creates me, presents me as complicated, complex, fascinating and difficult. My personality is lively, playful, challenging, deep and interesting. It feels like the most important part of me, it is my self creation. I have a big personality, take up a lot of room but without it I would still have a soul. Inside there is goodness. I have created a facade but under that there is a whole, healthy, loving, joyous spirit. I would still exist and would still be me.

Who am I without my consciousness—waking and in a dream? I am afraid I don't know what my consciousness is. Without consciousness it seems that there is no existence. To be conscious is to be alive, to be open, feeling, thinking, perceiving and in awareness of one's own existence. Without it I would be dead. Now what would it be like to be dead? I think it would be fine, to leave this state of consciousness and go on to nothingness. I once feared it beyond words, it was a night and day terror of mine to be dead, falling into the abyss, into infinity. But now, once again I look to mother's experience. She had a near death event at the time of my brother's birth. She said she walked toward the light, felt great peace and was being met by her dead father and other loved ones. If that is the beginning of death then I will embrace it. I do not long for it but I will welcome it when it comes. Without consciousness I might die, be nothing in body, move my spirit and energy into a new place.

LATER, LATER AND LATER: Tonight's practice was wonderful. I began by listening to a tape on the nature of ecstasy. Then I listened to wonderful music by Shlomo Carlbach that came from the Jewish ghettos of Europe. It reached into my collective unconscious and I reveled in the sounds of fiddles and flutes. I danced in ecstasy on the deck, in the full, red moonlight. I wept for the joy of having come to this place in me, of the joy of having peace in my heart and the beginning of a path that provides me with solace and hope. I danced and wept for surviving. I danced and wept for my father's family killed in the Holocaust. I danced and soared for having something in my heart besides the pain. I danced and wept for coming out of my crisis of the spirit and for doing it by myself,

rather than through the love of another, which I know can be removed at any time. I danced and wept for finding a new means for
growth. Therapy is not the answer for me any longer. I will not do it
and I will not go to it either. Therapy is not what reaches into the
soul, into the center nor into a level that I know can be reached. This
is a wonderful gift I gave to myself for my 50th birthday. It is far
better than any party I might have organized nor any interlude I
might have orchestrated. I gave myself me through this experience
and it is the best gift I could have given myself, I could not imagine
doing anything better nor more healthy.

REFLECTIONS AT MIDLIFE

Well, it is now three months later and the lessons I learned on that
mountain top are fairly well integrated. I still meditate every morning for at least an hour, using practices learned there as well as
employing other readings, chants and tapes that I have acquired.
The light and peace still surround me, although I see that there are
times when I can lose the centeredness I have achieved. It takes just
a very little time alone, breathing and finding that core, to come
back to myself once again. I have had to keep a small private
practice going, although I find myself turning away people or sug-
gesting that they go to the retreat center themselves. For the few
clients I have seen I try to teach them the practices I have picked up
in this short time. But I feel like a novice and I feel like a fake, when
I charge money to teach them how to find themselves. Perhaps one
day I will develop a practice that somehow utilizes these meditational and body work practices. However, until that time I feel that I
must continue to work on myself and then share what little I know
with those who are interested and ask. Otherwise I keep this experience quiet because I know that I have to go beyond my own ego and
the more I learn, the less I need to talk about it.

I understand that I have no control over what it is that happens to
me but that I can control how I respond to it. I understand that it is
my own thoughts that create my reality. But I do not believe in the
cognitive approach that speaks of changing those thoughts. I am
trying, truly trying, to go beyond ANY thoughts. I want to go to that

place between two thoughts and have that quiet, calm and absorbed space inside become my constant reality.

So how does this all relate to Kitzinger and Perkins, Heyward and Sandweiss? Well, it all comes together in my thoughts with a critique of psychotherapy as we know it. I know that many therapists employ relaxation techniques. Many also do body work and other non-traditional practices. However, what is missing, as I see it, is the connectedness and absorption of experience that is necessary for true change in a person. In my opinion it is not possible to find it in lesbian therapy or any other form of psychotherapy, as it is currently practiced. Kitzinger and Perkins argue that what is missing is the sense of community. We privatized human connection and made it a marketable commodity to be sold in a market place. We took away the revolutionary potential of lesbians by buying into the mistaken belief that therapy was the answer to all people's problems. They say that it is not therapy that is the answer and I concur. I have been afraid that if one became too spiritually oriented one might become apolitical and also lose any radical impulse. I see now the fallacy in that thinking. If one feels whole and at peace one can then engage in dealing with the inequities that surround us. Therapy might "cool" us out and depoliticize us but by using a spiritual practice in one's life there is plenty of room for radical action–in fact, one can then become energized to do more.

Heyward argues that the "boundaries betray us." I concur as well. As long as we establish the artificial, but necessary limits, given the way psychotherapy is constructed, we will always remain unconnected, even from the very therapists who should be helping us become connected. By this I mean that therapy should have been aiding us in feeling whole and at peace. Instead, because therapy is constructed as a business, with artificial limits placed on the relationship, it will always keep us from that which we are seeking. We are all looking for a sense of oneness with self and with other. Psychotherapy, today in the 1990s, cannot give us that. It is not created to provide that. Psychotherapy keeps us locked in our heads, in our behaviors, in our relationships. Instead, we are seeking a way back to our SELVES and psychotherapy, as I know it, does not have the slightest idea how to do that.

Sandweiss says that we need to find a guru, an avatar who can give us grace and help us on that journey. He tries to do it in his practice, with clients on a one-to-one basis. He uses quiet, dark, meditative rooms and he sits with them, as he would with others in contemplation in the ashram. This is admirable and hopefully he helps them find that which they are seeking. I think he is onto something, something that works for him and for his clients.

I know for myself, that I am still seeking the answer about how to integrate this knowledge into my work with people. Will I be a lesbian "paychotherapist," as I once was? I doubt it. Somehow I know there is no turning back to the cognitive, behavioral, depoliticized, isolated work I once did. For me what I will do may include spirituality, body work, chanting, meditating or just being quiet with people. What I hope to do is to find a way to continue my journey inward and help people find such a path as well. I also know I want to continue to talk and work with others who are also on such a path to find out what comes next, for all of us.

REFERENCES

Heyward, C. (1993). *When boundaries betray us: Beyond illusions of what is ethical in therapy and in life.* San Francisco: Harper San Francisco.
Kitzinger, C. and Perkins, R. (1993). *Changing our minds: Lesbian feminism and psychology.* New York: New York University Press.
Sandweiss, S. (1975). *Sai Baba: The holy man . . . and the psychiatrist.* San Diego: BirthDay Press.
Sandweiss, S. (1985). *Spirit and the mind.* Andhra Pradesh, India: Sri Satha Sai Books and Publications Trust.

After the Crash:
My Journey to Become a Lesbian
Feminist Body Psychotherapist

Lauree E. Moss

SUMMARY. This article chronicles the journey of a therapist and a lesbian feminist activist over the last thirty years. Her path has taken her through many different therapy experiences: Freudian psychoanalysis, Radical Psychiatry, encounter groups, women's groups, Gestalt Therapy, Feminist Therapy, Reichian Therapy, Bioenergetics, breath and movement therapy, and Integrative Body Psychotherapy (IBP). Synthesizing all she has experienced and studied, the author has developed Feminist Body Psychotherapy (FBP). Today her work integrates FBP with IBP, an approach similar to hers, which she experienced, studied and now teaches in Los Angeles. This article stresses the importance of integrating the body into psychotherapy to heal the mind-body split. *[Article copies available from The Haworth Document Delivery Service: 1-800-342-9678.]*

Lauree E. Moss, MSW, PhD, is a Board Certified Diplomate in Clinical Social Work, and a licensed clinical social worker in private practice in Santa Monica, CA. A founding member of The Feminist Therapy Institute, Inc., she contributed a chapter on body therapy to one of the Institute's books and edited a section on overlapping relationships between clients and therapists for another.

The author thanks Nancy Toder for her loving and painstaking editing; Alice Bloch for invaluable editing help; Jeanne Adleman for support and further editing; and Tari Sargent for typing the article through its many stages.

[Haworth co-indexing entry note]: "After the Crash: My Journey to Become a Lesbian Feminist Body Psychotherapist." Moss, Lauree E. Co-published simultaneously in *Women & Therapy* (The Haworth Press, Inc.) Vol. 18, No. 2, 1996, pp. 61-70; and: *Lesbian Therapists and Their Therapy: From Both Sides of the Couch* (ed: Nancy D. Davis, Ellen Cole, and Esther D. Rothblum) The Haworth Press, Inc., 1996, pp. 61-70; and: *Lesbian Therapists and Their Therapy: From Both Sides of the Couch* (ed: Nancy D. Davis, Ellen Cole, and Esther D. Rothblum) Harrington Park Press, an imprint of The Haworth Press, Inc., 1996, pp. 61-70. Single or multiple copies of this article are available from The Haworth Document Delivery Service [1-800-342-9678, 9:00 a.m. - 5:00 p.m. (EST)].

61

I was a twenty-year-old Latin major. The year was 1966. I was heterosexual, and very unhappy, though I did not know it. Junior year slump was experienced by many, I was told. Then a railroad train I was on derailed, and my life was totally altered. I thought I would die, and though obviously I survived, I became extremely depressed. I now had severe back pain, in addition to the migraine headaches that had started in my teens.

My parents and family doctor would not let me go back to school unless I saw a psychiatrist. This was my first experience in psychoanalytic psychotherapy. Dr. Mann was instrumental in facilitating insights about my life. However, he also became obsessed with my intense friendships with my "girlfriends." He repeatedly asked me whether I had sexual dreams about women. To my conscious knowledge, I never had. Of course, they then began.

BEGINNINGS: FROM FREUD TO FEMINISM TO REICH

After the crash, I switched my major to social psychology. Exploring my life and talking about my childhood unhappiness began to intrigue me. As a child, I was a "bed wetter" and a "thumb sucker," labels that caused me great shame and confusion. Through my studies and ongoing therapy, I learned about the effects of my emotionally absent and chronically ill mother and physically absent and emotionally unavailable father.

As I put it all together, I began to see how the pains of my childhood had shaped me. I focused on analyzing my dysfunctional family and trying to find a man, and suppressed my dreams about women. Dr. Mann was gleeful when I told him I was sleeping with Stan. When Stan and I broke up, Dr. Mann analyzed my resistance to marriage. Other psychiatrists later reinforced this view.

I felt defective, bad, and wrong. Something always compelled me to put my career first over my relationships with men. Perhaps it was seeing the marriages of my sisters, my aunts, my parents. I saw that marriage did not always work out like a storybook fantasy, but careers were lifelong.

In 1967 I began graduate studies in psychiatric social work, and entered psychoanalysis with a Freudian analyst. I desperately wanted to fit into the mold. I wanted to be a child psychoanalyst like Anna

Freud. I cannot express adequately the grief and pain I experienced in Freudian psychoanalysis. At least in face-to-face psychoanalytic therapy, my therapist had smiled at me and appeared to care. My Freudian analyst sat behind me. I lay on the couch. The little he said was always negative. He called me resistant when I wondered what he was thinking, or when I focused on political concerns. When I got mad at him, he interpreted this as rage at my father.

My depression deepened. I still had backaches, migraines, and frequent sinusitis. I was also diagnosed as having arthritis in my knees. This was exactly what had happened to my mother in her twenties. I was horrified, as my mother was now crippled with rheumatoid arthritis.

It was 1969, and I was 23, a social worker by day and a hippie by night. I worked in Detroit's first free clinic. I was now a member of the free love generation. I began to be aware of my attractions to women, but told no one.

I tried to find meaning in life. I had never been political. Now, the middle class norms I had lived by were being challenged. Were problems in our culture due to societal ills? Was I aiding the efforts to prop up a system that had no conscience? Any time I brought up these concerns in therapy, they were analyzed away.

I became more and more distressed, isolated, and lonely. My emotional state led me to take samples of drugs from the clinic. I was amassing a collection, which I planned to swallow eventually.

When I was at my lowest, wanting to die and not talking to anyone about it, a psychiatrist at the mental health institute where I worked took me to a conference on Radical Psychiatry. The speaker there addressed the very contradictions I felt. I became hopeful and excited about my life for the first time. I decided to live and flushed my pills down the toilet.

This was also the time of the Cambodia invasion and the Kent State killings. Some friends and I decided to participate in a demonstration in Washington protesting the slaying of four unarmed students by the National Guard. President Nixon came to the Lincoln Memorial in the early dawn hours before the demonstration to meet us, but refused to talk about issues. Hours later, I saw myself staring at Nixon in huge photographs on the front page of all the D.C. papers. "Nixon Greets Protesters," the headline declared. Not only was my picture in the D.C. papers, but it was in every paper across the nation. The picture blew my cover at work. For once, I didn't care.

In D.C. I met Larry. He was hitchhiking to Berkeley, having just dropped out of rabbinical school because of his radical political beliefs. He came to Detroit and then we traveled to Berkeley together and were married a few months later. However, after a couple of years, I was unable to remain committed to the marriage when it was put to the test of all my other commitments. I had finally gotten involved with the women's movement. What I was learning gave me tools to articulate my problem with Larry: I did not want to be a wife and mother. We finally parted amicably, and I did my own divorce.

In Berkeley I volunteered at the Free Clinic, where I was further exposed to the ideas of Radical Psychiatry. Depression was not just due to intrapsychic problems stemming from family and developmental delays and deficiencies. Instead, repression and depression were ways people adjusted to their environments. Changing involved facing repressed feelings and learning to identify and seek new options in one's life.

Within a year, I had become the co-director, with a friend, of the clinic's RAP Center. At the Center, we created a comfortable and relaxed environment. We did all our therapy and it was exciting. The ways I originally viewed therapy were changing drastically and quickly.

While working at the Berkeley Free Clinic, I began training in Gestalt Therapy, which provided an excellent framework for bringing the therapeutic dialog into the present. A great deal of emotion was expressed by both client and therapist, and there were none of the diagnostic labels that tended to pathologize clients.

The most important aspect of Gestalt Therapy for me was its focus on the body and body awareness. It was also the first time I had a female therapist and women trainers. They were invaluable to my newly developing feminist consciousness. Like me, these women were trying to integrate the lessons of feminism into their work. I began to feel quite powerful and alive.

At the clinic, I was also exposed to Bioenergetic Therapy. As a result, I experienced and trained in both Bioenergetic and Reichian therapy for about six years. These approaches showed me that psychosomatic illness and many physical problems can come from psychological stress residing in the body.

From these body therapies, I gained increased awareness of how my chronic muscular tension had kept such great pain in my body. These were excruciating experiences, but eventually my knees became pain-free and still are today. The ability to talk openly about my hurt and anger and to feel the power of these feelings in my body gave me an aliveness I had never experienced before. I began to understand the forces that foster the mind-body split. To connect feelings with the body, through breath, movement, and expression, became one of the basic elements of my own therapy as well as my therapy with clients.

Although I appreciated Reich's and Lowen's contribution in developing body therapies, I was also critical of their approaches. They often take as long and are as costly as psychoanalysis. They are also physiologically stressful forms of body therapy, employing breathing patterns that bring the body to a state in which the "patient" is forced to push through feelings. The exercises put a great deal of physical stress and strain on the structure of the body, and are often experienced as painful. Pain is considered necessary to help facilitate the release.

Additionally, use of words such as "patient" perpetuates the medical model of diagnosis and cure. Reich's and Lowen's approaches are also based on very traditional social values that do not permit new options for women's life choices. I was hurt by the blatant homophobia of my male therapists and trainers. Like many humanistic therapists at the time, they saw lesbianism as a "stage." They repeatedly inquired whether I was having sex with men. They also echoed Freud's belief that homosexuality was immature, that true mature genitality was possible only between a man and a woman.

My numerous attempts to educate my teachers about feminist principles and healthy homosexual behavior were useless. I eventually left those training and therapy experiences sad and angry, but also well-informed and eager to find alternatives.

Meanwhile, my experiences in women's consciousness groups and collectives were teaching me that sisterhood was powerful. I began to have words and concepts to explain and release feelings of depression and self-hate. I began to allow my feelings of love for my women friends to be expressed both emotionally and physically. After a year of bisexuality, I decided I was no longer interested in pursuing relationships with men. Relieved, I gave up any pretense of heterosexuality and came out publicly. Gradually, heterosexual colleagues, especially males, stopped referring to me.

ALTERNATIVES

In my search to find body therapy approaches that did not involve pain or stress and that were not homophobic, I studied and experienced many different modalities. The group of approaches I studied intensely for over six years were all developed by women. I have called them "A Woman's Way" (Moss, 1981). These approaches descended from a tradition developed by Elsa Gindler, whom I call "the grandmother" of body therapy. (Reich was often called "the grandfather.")

Elsa Gindler was a physical therapist renowned for her practice of a form of physical reeducation called "Gymnastik." This work, taught in Germany and Western Europe, integrated personal and physical development.

Gindler's work involved observing activities in daily life to see how breath is constricted while brushing the teeth, putting on socks, or eating. The goal was to awaken the senses. Through increased consciousness, Gindler believed, one could learn about one's self or core being. Gindler did not see pain as necessary for transformation. Her ideas resonated deep within me.

My personal work with women body therapists taught me how to accept myself on a deep inner level. I did not feel someone was working with me to get me to "open up," but rather to create the space to open. Two of my women body therapists, Marion Rosen and Doris Breyer, were especially supportive of my lifestyle and identity. With them I worked on my anger and pain from past experience with male therapists. My aching body had fewer and fewer days of pain. Eventually my migraines almost disappeared. I learned to love my body. Most important, I was learning about the connection between mind and body at deeper and deeper levels.

Because of my experiences with these women, I was learning new ways to work with clients. These techniques were diametrically opposed to the ones I learned in Bioenergetic and Reichian Therapy. Stressful exercises and positions were replaced with more gentle and playful moments. "Pushing through" was replaced with "allowing and sensing." Rather than intense breathing exercises, gentle breathing and awareness exercises were utilized. Deep physical pressure on tight musculature was replaced with gentle touch to promote the movement of energy through blocked areas.

FEMINIST BODY PSYCHOTHERAPY

In the late seventies, with other women, I had started a women's studies program at Esalen Institute in San Francisco, and in the eighties, a Graduate Program in Feminist Therapy at Antioch University/San Francisco, where I taught feminist therapy and body psychotherapy. Throughout these experiences, I participated as an open lesbian, which often required struggling with therapists and colleagues. During this time, I began developing my own approach, which I call Feminist Body Psychotherapy (FBP). FBP rejects the authoritarian medical model; it emphasizes nonpainful and nonstressful body therapy techniques within a feminist therapy framework. Each individual's process is viewed with respect and sensitivity.

FBP stresses the importance of understanding how the mind-body split contributes to the problems many women bring to therapy. Women often internalize their oppression and hold it in their bodies. One of the wonderful things about the body is that it doesn't lie. When treated with careful consideration, it will tell its own story and express the needs of the person with a direct, eloquent honesty.

As women recognize their needs, feel their bodies and the emotional blocks created by their early family and socialization experiences, symptoms begin to slip away. Repressed anger, inability to say no or set limits, inability to reach out and make contact, inability to experience pleasure during sex, all become less problematic as women experiment with new modes of behavior. When these conflicts can be consciously and physically addressed, the woman's creative, expressive energy and her ability to experience joy, excitement, and aliveness begin to emerge.

Another important issue for women is expression of our sexuality. Blocked expression of one's sexuality is usually centered around intimacy and trust in relationships. Causes can be lack of models or experience of healthy relationships, and/or the effects of childhood physical and sexual abuse. Inability to reach out for what one wants and disconnections between heart feelings and sexual feelings, often called the heart-genital split, are other issues that come up.

Sexuality is also connected to one's identity in the world. In Feminist Body Psychotherapy lesbian or bisexual identity is supported. Heterosexual women who are struggling to understand sexual feelings, whether toward women or toward men, are encouraged to explore all their feelings.

A feminist body psychotherapist also has to understand the special stressors associated with being lesbian in this culture. An exploration of whether the client's problems are due to internal dynamics, society, familial relations, or a combination, is essential to working effectively with lesbians. Covert and overt effects of homophobia have great impact on one's sexuality and self-concept.

The verbal therapy process of Feminist Body Psychotherapy is actually no different from any good therapy process. The therapist has to be able to form a relationship with her client that can tolerate both closeness and separateness, negative and positive feelings, and give the client a sense of being seen and understood.

INTEGRATIVE BODY PSYCHOTHERAPY

At the 1984 Advanced Feminist Therapy Institute conference in Oakland, I met my current lover. We had a long-distance relationship for one year, and then I moved to the Los Angeles area to live with her. This move took me away from my contacts in the San Francisco Bay area and my identity as a body psychotherapist. For many years in L.A., I did not practice or teach Feminist Body Psychotherapy directly, but always included body and breath awareness in my work with individuals and couples, and in supervision with therapists.

In my search for a body-oriented therapist with whom I could work in L.A., I located an old friend and teacher named Jack Rosenberg. He had developed, with Marjorie Rand, an approach called "Integrative Body Psychotherapy" (IBP). This work is described in a book called *Body, Self and Soul: Sustaining Integration* (1985).

After being in both individual and couple therapy from an IBP perspective, I decided to study the method. Over the last few years, I have become a certified IBP practitioner and teacher. Having a group of people to work with who are non-sexist and not homophobic has been an answer to my prayers.

IBP is similar to FBP in its integration of verbal methods with body therapy techniques. The developers were influenced by many of the same theorists as I. What is different about IBP is its integration of Object Relations Theory, infant development research, and Transpersonal Psychology. IBP also has a unique way of taking a client's history, called the "Primary Scenario," which investigates the relationship patterns of one's parents and grandparents to assess the effects they have had on an individual's relationships.

In IBP great emphasis is placed on the healing aspects of the therapeutic relationship. Like FBP, IBP does not use cathartic expression. Rather, clients are taught to experience aliveness in the body through learning how to develop an awareness of body sensations and feelings. Repressed memories, feelings, and longings often emerge through the breathing work. These are talked about and understood in the context of the client's life. As they are worked through, more feelings and energy can be experienced in the body.

When I developed Feminist Body Psychotherapy, I still used touch with my clients, as I knew only limited ways to teach women to work with themselves. However, I grew uncomfortable with touching my clients. Women began to see me because they heard I was a healer, and I did not want to be a healer. I was a psychotherapist who wanted to teach and model *self*-healing. I became more aware of the complicated messages transmitted by touch. For those of my clients who were survivors of physical and sexual abuse, touch brought up painful and confusing feelings.

IBP has resolved this dilemma for me, as it has developed a system of "self-release techniques" that almost replicate the techniques of FBP and other body psychotherapies. Clients, through the therapy process and by learning these ways of working on themselves can, in time, become their own healers.

I am forever moved by this quote from Adrienne Rich (1977), and I offer it in conclusion.

> In arguing that we have by no means yet explored or understood our biological grounding, the miracle and paradox of the female body and its spiritual and political meanings, I am really asking whether women cannot begin, at least, to think through the body. . . .
>
> We need to imagine a world in which every woman is the presiding genius of her own body. . . .
>
> This is where we have to begin. (pp. 290, 292)

REFERENCES

Falco, K. L. (1991). *Psychotherapy with lesbian clients: Theory into practice.* New York: Bruner/Mazel.

Lowen, A. (1975). *Bioenergetics.* New York: Coward, McCann and Geoghegan.

Moss, L. E. (1981). *A woman's way: A feminist approach to body psychotherapy.* Ann Arbor, MI: University Microfilms International.

Moss, L. E. (1985). Feminist body psychotherapy. In Rosewater, L. B., Walker, L. E. (Eds.). In *Handbook of feminist therapy: Women's issues in psychotherapy.* New York: Springer.

Reich, W. (1972). *Character analysis.* New York: Farrar, Straus, and Giroux.

Rich, A. (1976). *Of woman born.* New York: Bantam.

Rosenberg, J. L., Rand, M. L., and Asay, D. (1985). *Body self and soul: Sustaining integration.* Atlanta, GA: Humanics Limited.

Rush, A. K. (1973). *Getting clear: Body work for women.* New York: Random House.

Stern, D. N. (1985). *The interpersonal world of the infant.* New York: Basic Books.

Wyckoff, H. (1977). *Solving women's problems together.* New York: Grove Press.

Lesbian Clients/Lesbian Therapists:
Necessary Conversations

Sarah F. Pearlman

SUMMARY. There are multiple decisions and necessary conversations that are a crucial part of psychodynamic clinical practice between lesbian clients and lesbian therapists. These necessary conversations, which can make or break effective psychotherapy, include approach and timing of therapist disclosure of sexual orientation; boundary concerns; feelings which arise as the result of contact between therapist and client in lesbian social space; transference feelings; wishes for future friendship or lover relationship with the therapist; as well as conversations about these conversations. Necessary conversations also include those internal dialogues within the therapist so as to contain feelings and monitor behaviors when overidentification with lesbian clients occurs. *[Article copies available from The Haworth Document Delivery Service: 1-800-342-9678.]*

I have worked as a psychotherapist for nearly twenty years and have openly identified myself as a lesbian feminist therapist for fourteen of those years. I have also been publicly identified as a lesbian teacher in a variety of universities and colleges and have

---

Sarah Pearlman, PsyD, is a psychologist in private practice in Hartford, CT, and is currently teaching at the University of Hartford. She is an editor and author of articles in the anthology, *Lesbian Psychologies: Explorations and Challenges*, as well as other articles on lesbian relationships.

[Haworth co-indexing entry note]: "Lesbian Clients/Lesbian Therapists: Necessary Conversations." Pearlman, Sarah F. Co-published simultaneously in *Women & Therapy* (The Haworth Press, Inc.) Vol. 18, No. 2, 1996, pp. 71-80; and: *Lesbian Therapists and Their Therapy: From Both Sides of the Couch* (ed: Nancy D. Davis, Ellen Cole, and Esther D. Rothblum) The Haworth Press, Inc., 1996, pp. 71-80; and: *Lesbian Therapists and Their Therapy: From Both Sides of the Couch* (ed: Nancy D. Davis, Ellen Cole, and Esther D. Rothblum) Harrington Park Press, an imprint of The Haworth Press, Inc., 1996, pp. 71-80. Single or multiple copies of this article are available from The Haworth Document Delivery Service [1-800-342-9678, 9:00 a.m. - 5:00 p.m. (EST)].

taught many classes and training workshops on working with lesbian clients.

I would say that I have had minimal experiences as a lesbian client with heterosexual therapists. However, I do remember back to one incident during the 1960s while I was married and in therapy with a male psychiatrist (I was always in therapy during the time that I was married). What had happened was that I was driving to my weekly appointment, noticed a very attractive woman, and nearly drove my car into a telephone pole. I was very unnerved and couldn't understand why I was staring so intently at this woman—rather than at a man who was walking nearby. But, when I related all of this to my therapist, it was as if my words evaporated before they reached his ears. He did not respond, nor did he say a word, and so I was silenced and compliantly changed the subject and talked about other more meaningful events.

I never thought about my lesbianism as a problem. I mean being a lesbian was not the problem. It was the culture, the homophobia, the stigmatization, the responses and my reaction to the responses that made the problem. So that I was a lesbian was never my primary concern when I sought out therapy with lesbian therapists. However, it certainly emerged as a central issue when I needed to struggle with decisions about whether or how I should disclose in various and ongoing situations. And it did become the major issue when I decided to come out to my mother. First, I needed to talk about coming out to her and the reasons which had brought me to that point. And second, after I had told her I had to endure her reactions of anger and hurt, and learn to tolerate the many months of painful estrangement.

I want to add that being a lesbian therapist in supervised training with heterosexual supervisors did present some major difficulties. It placed me in situations of having to decide how and when to come out, and how I was going to educate particular supervisors on the subject of lesbianism (Lesbianism 101). I have needed to tolerate supervisors who did not comprehend the relational specifics of lesbian couples or take lesbian relationships very seriously. Nor did some of these supervisors understand the complexities of my coming out (or not coming out) to lesbian clients; or the smallness and confinements of lesbian communities, the strong likelihood that I would come into social contact with some of my clients, and that maintaining boundaries was a highly sensitive issue and a major concern.

Despite these hurdles, my style of clinical practice (psychodynamic) evolved over several years; shaped by my own experiences as a client in therapy (positive and negative); my particular experiences as a therapist; invaluable books and articles on therapy with lesbians, and inspiring conversations with other therapists—gay and straight. And as a lesbian therapist, I have some particular concerns and conceptualize and practice therapy in some very different ways with lesbian clients as compared to straight women clients.

THERAPY WITH LESBIAN CLIENTS: BEGINNING CONVERSATIONS

How I think about therapy with lesbian clients is that there are multiple decisions and necessary conversations that are a crucial part of psychodynamic clinical practice and that can make or break effective psychotherapy. When I first began to practice therapy, I would assume that most clients knew that I was a lesbian and would automatically confirm or disclose during the first session. However, I quickly learned that not all lesbian clients knew my sexual orientation, that the sexual orientation of a therapist was not always one's primary concern, and that different women had different feelings about working with a lesbian or heterosexual therapist. Moreover, I found that women who were at the beginning of the coming out (to self) process, in terms of questioning their sexual orientation, tended to want a therapist who could be truly neutral and not push in the direction of a lesbian identity. I learned also that some lesbians clearly preferred a heterosexual therapist who they believed could offer clearer boundaries and distance. That is, these women feared that they would not be able to contain romantic and/or sexual feelings towards a lesbian therapist and did not want to be concerned about the possibility of meeting their therapist in social spaces.

But, coming out to my clients is always an issue and at some point must be a conversation in therapy. First, because I am a fairly public lesbian, I have concerns that if a client learns that I am a lesbian from sources other than myself, she can experience a sense of betrayal so that therapy will be adversely affected. Also, because conversations in therapy are intimate, the relationship between client and therapist, although professional, is often one of closeness. Thus, when a client is talking about her life as a lesbian and does not know that my responses are based on my own personal experience as a lesbian, I feel uneasy and somewhat fraudulent until my sexual orientation is known.

I do believe that a therapist's personal life should be as private as possible. I also want to add that not all lesbian therapists have the professional option to come out, or to come out in all situations. However, I do think the fact of not coming out models secrecy and concealment with all of its various meanings. While I no longer disclose automatically during the first session unless it is clear that I have been sought out because I am a lesbian therapist, I think carefully about the timing of the coming out conversation. And I think very carefully about all of the related boundary concerns which are part of this conversation, and that are issues that heterosexual therapists do not have to confront.

There are many variables which determine approach and timing of the coming out conversation. Overall, I like to assess the degree of crisis or distress in that there may be more pressing concerns so that disclosure should be deferred. However, if this is not the case, my usual approach is to ask a series of questions like, "Have you thought about or wished to work with a lesbian therapist or a straight therapist?"; or "Does the sexual orientation of a therapist matter?" Responses to these questions let me know that the woman has deliberately sought me out as a lesbian therapist, or that she does not know that I am a lesbian, and/or that it may not be a concern.

If my client does not know that I am a lesbian, tells me that the sexual orientation of her therapist does not matter, and does not pursue the subject, I tend to wait until a later time to bring it up again. Then, at a later point in therapy (hopefully, there is a relevant conversation as lead-in), I might ask if she has thought that I might be a lesbian, or if she has been curious about this and wanted to ask me. And again, depending upon my client's response, I might invite her to ask me, or again wait to approach the subject.

Thus, I invite clients to ask me directly and then to tell me why they have not asked. I recall one client who told me that she was curious, but felt that "it was not her place" to ask. The phrase, "not her place" then became an important theme in therapy so that responses to these kinds of questions often provide important insights for both the client and myself. I ask my clients to tell me if they have concerns about my being a lesbian. And I ask them to talk about the conversation that we have just had. That is, we discuss the meanings that this conversation had for them, what feelings and thoughts were aroused, and what it would have been like if we did not have this conversation. In effect, this conversation models therapy, inviting questions, disclosures, and honesty; telling clients that I am interested in their feelings, in their thoughts about me and about me as a lesbian, and demonstrating that the conversation we are having is the kind of conversation we will be engaging in throughout therapy.

Once disclosure has occurred, I turn the conversation toward boundary issues and possible difficulties which need to be anticipated and addressed. The world of lesbian clients and lesbian therapists is very small, and I do not have the boundary luxury of privacy and anonymity that heterosexual therapists have (the closest counterpart is the heterosexual therapist who practices and lives in a small town or rural community). Because clients are often referred to me by previous or current clients, and because I write, engage in public speaking, and participate in community activities and events, clients often know something personal or professional about me and can have preconceived notions, expectations, and fantasies (beginning transference).

Therefore, there needs to be a conversation about "cross-over" or overlapping people that we both know (socially or other clients who are currently in therapy with me); and about what this brings up in terms of a client's particular feelings and fears; issues of trust; confidentiality; sharing other known people with one's therapist, and about how any or all of this might affect therapy. There needs to be a conversation about what we should do, and how we both might feel if and when we encounter each other in social spaces. That is, how should we behave? Should we say hello and stop to talk? Should we introduce the people we are with? What might she feel toward the person I'm with? What might we feel about the superficiality of the situation after the intimacy or closeness of therapy?

Finally, I tell clients that it will be important for us to talk about these social encounters afterwards as different feelings come up, and that the primary concern is that we continue talking honestly so that therapy is protected and remains effective.

I would say that boundaries are a very difficult part of my life as a therapist, and it has taken me a long time to fully understand that I do not own my life, that much of my privacy and freedom are curtailed and my social life circumscribed. Because lesbian therapists and clients inhabit and share a scarcity of lesbian public social space and because I now prefer to limit social contact with clients, I am more isolated when single and more reclusive when in relationship. I have learned to monitor my social behavior and to relate carefully with partners which includes containing affectionate behaviors, even in Provincetown (not unlike how lesbian couples monitor behavior in heterosexual space). Sharing social space with clients insures a degree of self-consciousness which I never expected to be part of my social world as I guess their reactions, hold back my own feelings, and anticipate the necessary conversations which we will be having in subsequent therapy sessions.

Social encounters between therapist and client affect therapy in that the more I am known as a person, the more clients become concerned with feelings toward me and with how I feel and think about them so that therapy becomes "therapist-directed," self-esteem and protection of narcissism become issues and can block self-awareness and honesty in the therapy interaction. Clients can be reluctant to talk about shame and other negative feelings about lesbianism with a lesbian therapist; or they may want to be viewed as a "good" lesbian, that is, a political lesbian if they believe the therapist is political. Unless discussed, these concerns can result in clients' false and compliant behaviors, or editing and omitting feelings, thoughts, and experiences which are considered negative so as to present themselves in a positive or "healthy" light and protect self-image and self-esteem.

IDENTIFICATIONS AND INTERNAL CONVERSATIONS

One important aspect of working with lesbian clients is my strong identification, and sometimes overidentification (counter-transference) with these women. While many of their growing-up and identity development histories are different from my own, since I came out in a political context and at a later age, their stories often touch on mine and I share many of their experiences and struggles.

Therapy with lesbian clients means helping these women to manage the often overwhelming social costs when love and desire between women are outlawed and threaten patriarchal privilege of domination and sexual control. Therapy with lesbians means hearing shame (internalized homophobia) and listening to life stories of ongoing vigilance, careful secretiveness, and expert conversational editing. It means listening to fears of losing one's children; the need to placate divorcing or ex-husbands; the consequences of coming out; the abbreviated conversations, and relationships reduced to polite superficialities when one's life as a lesbian is outside the range of comfortable discussion. It means being a witness to a multiplicity of losses, traumas, and fears as I hear about rejection by parents; restricted contact with nieces and nephews; fears of loss of income; work discriminations; legal threats; street harassment; and sometimes, financial disinheritance. It means listening to the complexities of lover and friendship relationships; the heterosexual rituals and celebrations while many years of a committed lesbian relationship remain illicit and unaffirmed, and the feelings of being outside the "normal" heterosexual world; marginalized, and invisible. I hear about ex-lover aftermath; about absence of sexual desire and activity; about gender and femininity concerns; and about community politics, political correctness and exclusion, and the longing for connection.

My identification with these women means that I can deeply understand and am quickly able to clarify feelings and the undertow of possible meanings to events and interactions. I am also able to validate and normalize their perceptions, the appropriateness of their reactions and responses to homophobia, and the cost of their choice to live as lesbians as well as its rewards. However, listening to these stories is also like listening to my own life as a lesbian as they stir my memories and provoke my own internal dialogue or conversation. And I must subdue my own feelings of sorrow, indignation, and rage at what I, along with my clients (many of whom I think of as perfectly wonderful), have to endure because of how we wish to live, and who we love and desire.

It is at these times that I must have a conversation with myself in order to contain and make another kind of boundary, one between these women's feelings and my own. This means halting my often overwhelming inclinations to rush in, to protect, overprotect, and rescue in order to make their feelings (and my own) disappear. At other times, I have to stop my intellectualized explanations on the social determinants or politics of heterosexism; interventions which silence my clients and dilute their feelings. Still at other times, my identification with clients will affect my listening and I become so caught up in the woman's story that I lose perspective, miss the deeper damage and vulnerability, and forget that more carefully thought out responses and a differently structured therapy might be needed.

However, my identification with lesbian clients also means that I experience feelings of pride when I hear the devotion to friendship, the loyalty to ex-lovers, and the struggle to maintain old connections as well as to make new ones. In addition, I feel pride in these women (and myself) for their integrity, their brave choice to live authentic lives, and their strength and ability which has enabled them to tolerate, manage, recover, and survive the various costs, and to locate the joys and rewards.

OTHER CONVERSATIONS

There are many other conversations that take place between lesbian clients and therapists. There are conversations when a woman would realize that my questions were not about why she was a lesbian, or what went wrong, but that I wanted to understand her feelings and the meanings she had attached to certain life experiences. Or there are conversations when a particular woman would tell me that it was not my intellectual or political interventions, or even my insights, which were helpful, but rather that I had responded in ways that indicated I cared about her and how she felt about herself.

However, the conversation most often concealed or disguised that weaves its way throughout therapy between lesbian client and lesbian therapist is the necessary conversation about the many meanings the therapist has for the client, who she symbolizes, and the feelings the client may experience toward her. Feelings toward therapists originate in the intensely personal, intimate, nurturant, and idealizing connection between therapist and client and bypass the "real" therapist. That is, clients do not truly know their therapists as real people in real, complex, and mutual relationships. Rather, clients know therapists as an idealized combination of a real person and a person who is in a therapeutic and non-mutual role; a role which provides boundaries and finiteness and so allows the therapist to possess, represent, and offer her clients the qualities of non-judgementalness, objectivity, patience, and undemanding and unconditional responsivity that are at the core of therapeutic interaction.

Clients can experience love, rage, hate, envy, or dependency as therapists become older sisters, mothers, fathers, or wished-for lovers. Clients can hope for future friendship, harbor romantic fantasies, experience sexual desire, and fall in love with their therapists. However, these conversations, when a client bravely takes the risk to tell me her feelings toward me, and that she wants to be my friend or lover, are often the most difficult in therapy for both myself and my client. They expose feelings, must result in the refusal of the client's wishes, and so risk rejection; and these are the times when I feel most confused, clumsy, and ineffective in therapy. These conversations mean that I must listen to my client's feelings of love or desire, yet contain my own reactions, such as embarrassed pleasure. And I must refuse to do or to be what the client is telling me she wishes; and yet respond in a way which will neither deny or invalidate her feelings, nor injure her emotionally and cause her to feel shame.

So I must find words for this conversation of refusal. Words which will tell my client that I am her therapist which means that I must be a good therapist, and that I am there not to do her harm nor create possibilities for future hurt or rejection. But that I am there to protect our therapy, so that I cannot be her friend or lover, now or later when therapy has ended. And I must find the words to help her understand the reasons and the basis for my refusal. Reasons which I must express, not as my personal disinclination or in clinical jargon, but that originate out of my own lived experience and resulting firm beliefs.

These conversations resolve in relief for some clients, but will cause anger, hurt, and shame for others. Yet, it is also a conversation that must continue as I ask clients to tell me what this conversation has meant, how she now feels toward me as a result of this conversation, what would have happened if we did not have this conversation, and what it might connect to in terms of other people and her history of other wishes and refusals. It is a conversation which will also emerge and reemerge throughout therapy as I watch for changes in connection and how my client and I are interacting.

There are many advantages when a lesbian client works with a lesbian therapist. For the lesbian client, these advantages include shared experiences and understandings, and the opportunity to identify with and idealize another lesbian as a role model. For myself as a lesbian therapist, it gives me the opportunity to offer my respect for my clients' integrity and authenticity, to affirm their relationships and relationship struggles, and to accept their idealization of me as a role model. It allows me both privilege and joy to enter so many personal worlds, to be a part of lessening pain, and increasing authentic self-acceptance and pride, as well as to learn once again that change within therapy lodges over time and in the repeated experience of feeling deeply heard, cared about, and respected by a loved or idealized therapist.

BIBLIOGRAPHY

Boston Lesbian Psychologies Collective (1987). *Lesbian psychologies: Explorations and challenges.* Urbana: Univ. of Illinois Press.

Burch, B. (1993). *On intimate terms: The psychology of difference in lesbian relationship.* Urbana: Univ. of Illinois Press.

Burch, B. (1993). Heterosexuality, bisexuality, and lesbianism: Rethinking psychoanalytic views of women's sexual object choice. *Psychoanalytic Review,* 80(1), 83-99.

Greenberg, D. (1989). *The construction of homosexuality.* Chicago: The Univ. of Chicago Press.

Isay, R. (1989). *Being homosexual.* NY: Farrar, Strauss, Giroux.

Krestan, J. & Bepko, C. (1980). The problem of fusion in the lesbian relationship. *Family Process, 9,* 287-289.

O'Connor, N. & Ryan, J. (1993). *Wild desires and mistaken identities: Lesbianism and psychoanalysis.* NY: Columbia Univ. Press.

Rothblum, E. & Cole, E. (1989). *Lesbianism: Affirming non-traditional roles.* NY: The Haworth Press, Inc.